MORE THAN **400**
AMAZING COLOR
PHOTOS THROUGHOUT
THE BOOK!

NATIONAL
GEOGRAPHIC
KiDS

ULTIMATE REPTILE-OPEDIA

CHRISTINA WILSDON

THE MOST COMPLETE REPTILE REFERENCE EVER

NATIONAL GEOGRAPHIC
WASHINGTON, D.C.

CONTENTS

INTRODUCTION

Reptiles of all kinds creep, crawl, and slither through the pages of *Ultimate Reptileopedia*—from tiny lizards that can perch on a penny to snakes that are nearly as long as a bus. You'll also meet flying geckos, turtles as big as boulders, snakes that play dead, lizards that run on water, and chameleons that change color in an instant. The amazing reptiles that share our world represent one of Earth's oldest and most successful forms of life. The first reptiles roamed Earth about 315 million years ago—long before those famous reptiles known as dinosaurs ruled the planet. Today, reptiles live nearly everywhere but in the coldest regions. Some of them, such as house geckos, are even at home indoors.

The more you learn about reptiles, the more you want to find out. They boast a variety of adaptations that make them endlessly amazing and often downright weird! The sharp prickles of the thorny devil lizard, for example, are not just a suit of armor—they also are grooved so that water trickles down them right to the lizard's mouth. Another lizard, the chuckwalla, puffs itself up like a balloon so it can't be pulled out of rock crevices by a predator. A snake called the bandy-bandy forms hoops and loops with its body to look scary. And just when you think you've seen it all, scientists discover new reptiles—or find out new things about known species, such as the sneaky hunting technique of the tentacled snake!

Writing *Ultimate Reptileopedia* allowed me to blend my interest in animals with reading and researching all about them. I enjoyed spending time with reptiles—from alligators to zebra-tailed lizards, and I hope you will, too!

Christina Wilsdon

I grew up in the mountains of West Virginia, U.S.A., surrounded by nature. One of my favorite hobbies was fishing, but I was raised to fear snakes and other reptiles. As a result, I spent my boyhood in fear of these fascinating animals. It wasn't until I enrolled in a tenth-grade biology class that I learned to appreciate reptiles for their beauty and importance in the big picture of nature. I discovered that they are important predators that help maintain a keen balance in the natural world by feeding on insects, rodents, and other creatures.

I went on to major in biology in college and subsequently earned a master's degree and a Ph.D. in my field of study: reptiles (which is known as herpetology). Recently I retired after 51 years of teaching, mostly at the college level. My greatest delight in teaching was the numerous hours I spent in the field with students searching for reptiles (and amphibians). What a joy it was to watch students who, like me, once had a fear of reptiles, or others who didn't initially know much about them, become "hooked" on herpetology.

Now many of my students teach others about reptiles throughout the United States. When I was asked to review *Ultimate Reptileopedia*, I hesitated at first because I was concerned that, given the enormous biodiversity of reptiles on our planet, I wouldn't know them all. What I found was that I had to do some research of my own and, as a result, I learned some very interesting facts about reptiles. There is always new information to discover about them!

As you read this encyclopedic book, I hope you will become as excited about reptiles as I am, mesmerized by their mystery and majesty.

Thomas K. Pauley, Ph.D.

HOW TO USE THIS BOOK

Ultimate Reptileopedia **is filled with just about anything and everything you'll want to know about reptiles.**

The first section, "Discovering Reptiles," is an introduction to these amazing animals. It will help you learn about and understand them, so that when you read the profiles of individual reptiles, you'll already know a lot about them in general. Reptile Senses is one of the topics explored in the first section.

The second section, the main part of the book, features profiles of different reptile species. The profiles are organized by the reptile order to which each belongs, starting with the order with the most species. That order is Squamata, which includes lizards, snakes, and amphisbaenians (also known as worm lizards). The other orders are Testudines (turtles and tortoises); Crocodylia (crocodiles, alligators, caimans, and gharials); and Rhynchocephalia (the tuatara).

There are 91 full profiles of reptile species in the book. Here is an example of one of them.

In each species profile, you'll find a section that gives you fast facts about that species. You can find out at a glance how large it is, what it eats, where it can be found, and the kind of habitat in which it lives. And you'll see its scientific name as well as other common names it may have.

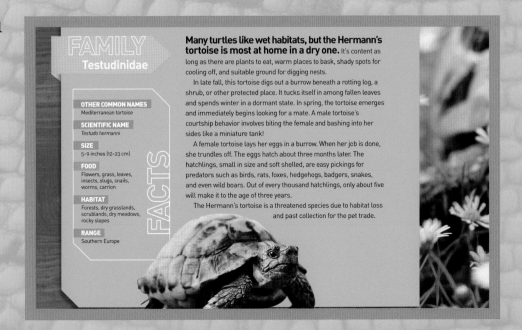

DISCOVERING REPTILES

WHAT IS A REPTILE?

When you think about what a "reptile" is, what comes to mind? Maybe you picture a lizard sunning itself on a stone wall, or a snake slithering in the grass. Perhaps you imagine a turtle paddling in a pond, or an alligator lurking in a marsh. Maybe you even think, "Dinosaur!"

These animals are very different from each other, but they are all reptiles (yes, even the dinosaur) because they are all animals that have a backbone, lungs for breathing air, and skin that is partly or completely covered with scales.

You can often quickly tell whether an animal is a reptile or not. Reptiles don't have hair, as mammals do. They don't have six legs, like insects do. And they don't have fins and breathe underwater with gills, as fish do.

But some animals might puzzle you. What, for example, is a salamander? With its four skinny legs and pointy tail, it *looks* like a lizard. Look closely, though, and you'll see it doesn't have scales. That's because it's an amphibian, not a reptile. Salamanders, frogs, and other amphibians don't have scaly skin.

Many other differences separate reptiles and amphibians. Reptiles, for example, can lay eggs in many habitats on land—even in very dry places, such as deserts. Their eggs have tough shells that resist drying out. Amphibians, however, lay jellylike eggs that dry out easily. Their eggs need to be in water or moist places. In addition, most amphibian hatchlings go through a larval stage before growing into their adult forms (think of those legless, fishlike frog babies called tadpoles). Reptiles start life with all four legs and look a lot like their parents, only smaller, as soon as they're born.

This red salamander looks like a reptile. What you can't see is that on the inside, it doesn't have any lungs! It breathes directly through its skin. Even amphibians with lungs have this ability. Amphibian eggs can also exchange oxygen and carbon dioxide directly with the air. Water can seep into and out of them, too.

Reptiles and amphibians are both studied by the same scientists. Scientists who study reptiles or amphibians are called herpetologists. *Herpeto* comes from a Greek word that means "creeping thing."

SCIENTIFIC CLASSIFICATION

Scientists divide animals into groups to help our understanding. Here's how one lizard species, the common flat lizard (seen left), gets grouped.

Kingdom: Animalia (animals)

Phylum: Chordata (animals with backbones)

Class: Reptilia (reptiles)

Order: Squamata (scaled reptiles)

Family: Cordylidae (girdled lizards)

Genus: *Platysaurus* ("flat, wide lizard")

Species: *intermedius* ("in between")

REPTILE TYPES

Scientists have named and described nearly 10,000 kinds, or species, of reptiles. This number, however, changes from year to year. Extinction, for example, can cause numbers to drop. But changes also occur due to the ongoing discovery of new reptile species.

In 2010, for example, scientists revealed the discovery of a human-size, fruit-eating monitor lizard in the Philippines. How could anybody overlook a reptile like that? Surprisingly easily! It lives high in the treetops of remote mountainside forests. Filipino people, however, were quite familiar with it. They called it the *bitatawa* and had long hunted it for food. In fact, that's how scientists first learned about its existence—they saw it in a photograph of hunters and their prey that was snapped in 2001. Nearly ten years passed, however, before researchers found an actual lizard in the wild.

Sometimes researchers even rediscover a reptile thought to be extinct. That's what happened in 2005 when a long-nosed lizard called the horned anole was photographed in Ecuador. Scientists thought it had gone extinct because nobody had seen one for about 40 years.

The number of species also grows when scientists figure out that one species is really two or even more species. These "new" species are often revealed when

DIVERSITY OF THE ANIMAL KINGDOM

INVERTEBRATES 95.6%

FISH 2.2%

BIRDS 0.7%

REPTILES 0.6%

AMPHIBIANS 0.5%

MAMMALS 0.4%

What do scientists do after they figure out what's what? They place the reptiles into groups called orders. All living things are organized in this way. Reptiles are divided into four orders. The percentages of reptiles by order are noted below.

ORDER SQUAMATA:
lizards, snakes, and worm lizards (amphisbaenians)
96.3%

ORDER TESTUDINES:
turtles and tortoises
3.4%

ORDER CROCODYLIA:
crocodiles, alligators, caimans, and gharials
0.3%

ORDER RHYNCHOCEPHALIA:
the tuatara
0.01%

PERCENTAGE OF VERTEBRATES BY GROUP

- **FISH** 55%
- **BIRDS** 16%
- **REPTILES** 12%
- **MAMMALS** 8%
- **AMPHIBIANS** 5%
- **HAGFISH & OTHER PRIMITIVE VERTEBRATES** 4%

scientists use computer programs and other new technology to analyze animals' genes—the chemical codes that contain instructions for "building" living things.

In the past, scientists classified animals by studying their body structures inside and out. Animals with much in common, they figured, were probably closely related. Animals that shared fewer traits were likely not as closely related. Today, scientists still use these observations, but they also employ modern technology.

Computers and other tools let scientists look at genes, cellular structures that are special to each species. This deeper study reveals more about how animals are related, how they change over time, and what their ancestors are. It has even given us clues to how birds appear to be reptiles, too!

Birds are warm-blooded animals, but they descended from dinosaurs called theropods. As a result, some scientists put birds in a fifth reptile order called Dinosauria. Other scientists think Dinosauria is a class that contains birds, dinosaurs, and ancient reptiles called therapsids. And while some scientists study bird-dinosaur links, others dig even more deeply into the past to find out about reptiles that lived before dinosaurs.

ANCIENT REPTILES

The first reptiles began roaming Earth more than 300 million years ago. These early reptiles were closely related to the ancestors of modern mammals.

About 230 million years ago, the reptiles known as dinosaurs evolved. They were the dominant form of life on land until about 65 million years ago. This "Age of Reptiles" came to a sudden end when a giant asteroid smacked into Earth on Mexico's Yucatán Peninsula, causing huge fires, earthquakes, landslides, and tsunamis (tidal waves) and plunging the planet into darkness. Dinosaurs as well as marine reptiles and pterosaurs (flying reptiles) went extinct, while smaller reptiles and many other animals survived.

Dinosaurs aren't the ancestors of modern reptiles, but they are related. Crocodylians are their closest "cousins" because dinosaurs and crocs shared a common ancestor: a croc-like creature that belonged to a group of animals called "thecodonts" or "basal archosaurs." Lizards, snakes, amphisbaenians, and the tuatara share an even more ancient ancestor with dinosaurs and crocodiles. That ancestor was a reptile-like amphibian that lived long before thecodonts did.

What about turtles? Scientists are still figuring out where turtles belong in reptile history. Turtles have existed since the time of dinosaurs. Scientists placed them on a branch of the family tree that splits off from other reptiles very early in reptile history. Today, some scientists suggest turtles may actually be closely related to crocodylians and birds, while others focus on connections they may have with lizards.

One of the oldest turtle fossils ever found is about 210 million years old. It was big—about a yard (1 m) long. It could not pull its head into its shell, but it had spikes on its neck and tail for protection.

m/monstersnake

The ongoing discovery of new fossils keeps scientists busy! One recent find revealed fossils of a giant South American snake that lived about 60 million years ago. This snake, *Titanoboa*, weighed more than 2,000 pounds (907 kg) and was about 45 feet (13.7 m) long!

The tuatara's ancestors scampered among dinosaurs 200 million years ago. Today, this lizardlike animal is the only species of its kind. It lives only in New Zealand.

ARE REPTILES COLD-BLOODED?

Cold-blooded. **You'll often see this chilling phrase when you read about reptiles.** They are often described as cold-blooded animals, while mammals and birds are called warm-blooded. But what exactly do the terms mean?

A cold-blooded animal has a body temperature that changes according to the temperature around it. Its body does not generate lots of heat as does the body of a warm-blooded animal such as you. Heat is produced in a warm-blooded animal's body as it digests food, moves its muscles, and carries out other bodily processes. A reptile's body doesn't give off large amounts of heat in this way.

Most warm-blooded animals such as mammals and birds also have outer coverings that help slow heat loss from their bodies. A mammal's fur and a bird's feathers provide excellent insulation.

A reptile, however, doesn't have fur or feathers to hold on to heat and keep out cold. As a result, its blood temperature can drop very low on a cold day and shoot up quickly on a hot day.

A reptile can actually run the risk of being too "hot-blooded" on a sunny day in the desert. That's one reason why scientists don't use the term "cold-blooded." It's not accurate because a reptile's blood isn't cold all the time. If it were, a reptile would not be able to slither, run, climb, or even digest its food.

A "cold-blooded animal" is more properly called an ectotherm. An ectotherm is an animal that uses its surroundings to heat up and cool down its body. "Ecto" means "outside" and "therm" means "heat." An animal that makes its own body heat is called an endotherm—"endo" means "inside."

So how do reptiles control their body temperature if their bodies don't make heat? Turn the page to find out!

A bird is an endotherm. Its body makes its own heat. By fluffing its feathers, a bird traps a layer of air that slows heat loss from its body. A reptile lacks this kind of insulation.

Being "cold-blooded" has one big advantage over being "warm-blooded": An ectothermic animal doesn't burn energy producing body heat. A big crocodile, for example, can go for months without eating. An endothermic animal can't do this because it needs food to supply fuel for heat production.

Some reptiles have the ability to use an endothermic strategy: They shiver so their muscles produce body heat. Some female pythons shiver to make heat that keeps their eggs warm.

WARMING UP, KEEPING COOL

A reptile doesn't pump out body heat like an endotherm, but it can definitely control its body temperature. Management of body temperature is called thermoregulation. A reptile thermoregulates mainly by moving back and forth between warm places and cool ones.

A lizard basking on a wall is using the sun's heat to warm its body. It's also soaking up heat from the warm stone beneath it. Maybe you've seen turtles basking on a log in a pond, or a snake basking on sun-baked pavement.

After it's heated up, a reptile gets busy looking for food, patrolling its territory, or finding a mate, if it's mating season. If the day is hot, it avoids overheating by finding a cool place to hang out. It may retreat to a shady spot, slip into a crevice, hide in a cool burrow, or take refuge in water.

Shady places and burrows aren't easy to find if you live in a sandy desert. But desert reptiles have other ways to chill out. Many desert lizards, snakes, and turtles lie low during the hot day and come out only at night, when it's cooler.

Hanging out underground is a great way to escape a desert's heat. On a hot day, the ground may be a scorching 170°F (77°C). A few inches below the surface, however, it may be a comfortable 80°F (27°C).

The shovel-snouted lizard lives on the scorching hot sands of the Namib Desert in southern Africa. To beat the heat, it stands on just two of its feet while holding up the other two to let them cool off. Then it quickly switches, putting the cool feet back on the sand and lifting up the two hot feet.

Reptiles that live in places with cold winters avoid freezing temperatures by hibernating. Snapping turtles tuck themselves into the muddy bottoms of ponds and lakes to ride out the winter. Snakes curl up under rocks, log piles, and the like.

A marine iguana feeds in chilly ocean waters. It basks on sun-warmed lava rocks to raise its temperature both before and after swimming. Its dark color helps absorb the sun's warmth.

SCUTES AND SCALES: REPTILE SKIN

Have you ever shuddered at the thought of holding a snake? You might think that snakes will feel slimy and gross. But snakes, like other reptiles, are anything but slimy. Their skins are dry and covered with scales. A snake actually feels cool and silky!

The outermost layer of a reptile's skin is called the epidermis. It's made of a tough material called keratin. This is the same substance that forms your nails, hair, and skin. A reptile's scales are thick spots of keratin, with thinner areas in between that allow the skin to flex and bend. They may overlap each other, like shingles on a roof, or sit separately, like bricks in a path.

Keratin also covers sturdy scales called scutes that cover most turtles' shells. And it's found in the bony armor of crocodylians and other reptiles that grow bony plates. These plates are called osteoderms. Osteoderms are produced in an inner layer of skin called the dermis. They contain a base of bone covered with fibers of keratin.

Reptiles periodically shed the outer layer of their skin. Shedding, or molting, is necessary because a growing reptile needs a larger suit of armor. Young reptiles grow quickly, so they shed more often than adult reptiles do. (Reptiles continue to grow all their lives, but the growth rate is much slower in adults.) Shedding also gets rid of worn-out or otherwise damaged skin. Lizards shed their skin in patches, while snakes shed their skin all at once. They crawl right out of it, leaving an inside-out snakeskin behind. Turtles and tortoises shed in patches from their limbs, neck, and tail and also from their scutes.

A SNAKE SHEDS ITS SKIN

1

A snake getting ready to shed has dull skin and looks as if it has blue eyes. That's because a cloudy, oily fluid fills the space between the old skin and the new skin forming under it.

2

The snake rubs its snout on rocks or other surfaces to loosen the skin and get the shedding process going. Then it crawls to peel off the skin, much as you might remove a sock by rubbing your foot on a carpet.

3

The snake's new skin is bright and shiny, but the shed skin is colorless.

Osteoderms in an alligator's back protect its internal organs from damage if it's attacked by another 'gator. Crocodylians are incredibly well armored. Some species even have bony eyelids!

LIVING COLOR

What color crayon would you grab if you decided to draw a reptile? Chances are you'd go for green or brown. Lots of reptiles are green or brown because these colors help them blend in with leaves, bark, and rocks. But you'd better have a 64-pack of crayons handy, because reptiles also come in colors such as turquoise blue, lemon yellow, and hot pink. These bright colors are often displayed in stripes, bands, and spots in intricate patterns.

A reptile's color is contained in its second layer of skin, the dermis. Its colors are created by different color cells called chromatophores. The color on a patch of skin depends on the sizes and numbers of different chromatophores.

Some chromatophores contain red or yellow pigments. Others contain a pigment called melanin. Melanin produces shades of light brown, yellow-brown, dark brown, and black in reptiles and other vertebrates, including humans. Different mixtures of these shades produce different colors.

How the melanin is distributed affects color, too: If it is spread throughout cells, it makes an area dark, but if it's clumped in the center of each cell, it makes an area pale.

What about that most famous reptile color, green? A reptile's chromatophores don't contain green pigments—or blue or white ones, either. These colors are created by chromatophores called iridophores, which don't contain pigment. Instead, they hold crystal-like substances that reflect light and break it up into the colors of the rainbow. Blue light reflected by these cells, for example, blends with the skin's yellow pigments to make green.

This Gaboon viper almost disappears among dead leaves, thanks to its brown-and-black pattern. It's a good example of how color can help a reptile hide in plain sight—a trick called camouflage.

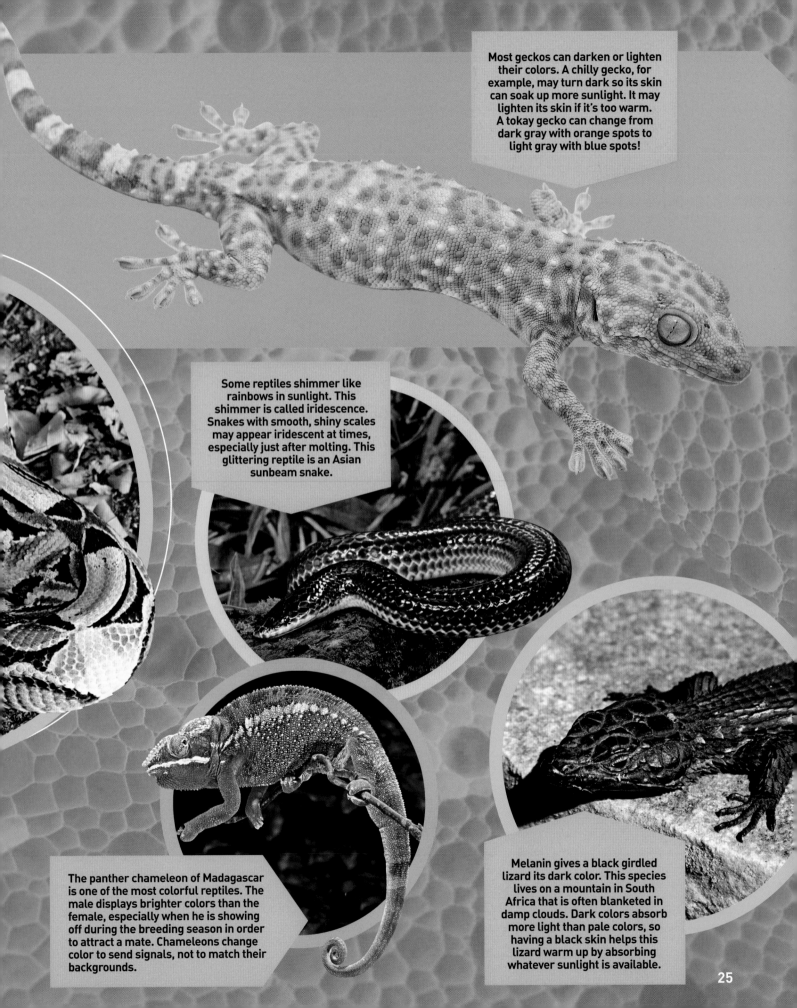

Most geckos can darken or lighten their colors. A chilly gecko, for example, may turn dark so its skin can soak up more sunlight. It may lighten its skin if it's too warm. A tokay gecko can change from dark gray with orange spots to light gray with blue spots!

Some reptiles shimmer like rainbows in sunlight. This shimmer is called iridescence. Snakes with smooth, shiny scales may appear iridescent at times, especially just after molting. This glittering reptile is an Asian sunbeam snake.

The panther chameleon of Madagascar is one of the most colorful reptiles. The male displays brighter colors than the female, especially when he is showing off during the breeding season in order to attract a mate. Chameleons change color to send signals, not to match their backgrounds.

Melanin gives a black girdled lizard its dark color. This species lives on a mountain in South Africa that is often blanketed in damp clouds. Dark colors absorb more light than pale colors, so having a black skin helps this lizard warm up by absorbing whatever sunlight is available.

QUICK-CHANGE ARTISTS!

Reptiles that change color have the ability to change the size of their color cells. If their red cells swell up, their skin turns red. Likewise, the yellow cells swell up to turn skin yellow. The cells can also shrink, which lets light bounce off the cells that reflect blue and white.

Melanin can also be moved around in the skin to make it darker and lighter. Melanin-containing cells have fingerlike tentacles called dendrites that lace through the skin. Melanin spreads through skin by trickling into these dendrites, which makes skin darker. When the melanin seeps out of the dendrites and clumps back inside the melanin cells, the skin turns pale.

Together, these colors mix to produce a wide range of hues, turning the reptile into a living kaleidoscope. The ability to change colors is widespread among lizards. Anoles, for example, can switch back and forth between brown and green, and chameleons can go from being pale green to looking like a rainbow-hued neon sign in less than a minute.

Color changes can help lizards communicate. Chameleons, for example, use color changes in mating behavior. A male flashes bright colors to lure a female. A female who's already carrying eggs will adopt colors that send the message "Babies on board—go away!"

A few snakes are able to change their body color over the course of a day. The Haitian wood snake, for example, is dark by day. At night, it can turn yellow with green, red-brown, and black markings.

Many lizards have skin that darkens to help them absorb sunlight and warm up. That's because dark colors don't reflect as much light as pale colors do. A green iguana, for example, may turn dark green. But it may turn pale to reflect light if it's sitting in direct sunlight in the middle of the day.

The central bearded dragon of Australia has a spiky "beard" that it spreads open when it's angry. A male's beard turns black when he's flaring it aggressively at another male.

HOW REPTILES "TALK"

Ask a friend what a dinosaur sounds like, and he'll probably roar.

Ask him what a reptile sounds like, and you'll probably get a puzzled look. Reptiles aren't famous for making a lot of noise. Some species, however, do use sounds to communicate. Reptiles also communicate with signals, movements, color, and smells.

Making Noise: The best known reptilian sound-makers are geckos. Geckos are the only lizards with vocal cords. A male tokay gecko loudly cries "To-kay!" when it is looking for a mate. Male barking geckos sit at the entrances of their burrows in African deserts and yip.

But reptiles without vocal cords make sounds, too. Many snakes, lizards, and turtles hiss when they feel threatened. So do crocodiles and alligators, who also roar, bellow, and rumble. Baby crocodylians call to their mother with peeps, squeaks, and chirps.

Body Language: Visual signals and body language play the largest role in reptile communication. Many lizards, for example, bob their heads, puff up their bodies, and do push-ups to threaten other lizards. Chameleons, which once were thought to change color only to match their background, actually use color changes mainly to signal aggression and interest in mating.

Telltale Smells: Reptiles appear to use scent to communicate, too. Studies show that some species, such as wall lizards, use scents to mark territory. Female garter snakes emit smells that attract male snakes during mating season.

Body language speaks loudly in the world of reptiles. If two male tuataras meet, for example, they both open their mouths wide—a behavior called gaping. The first tuatara to shut his mouth is basically saying, "I give up. You win!"

Is this bearded dragon waving to a friend? Giving a high five? Raising its hand in class? None of the above. Waving a foreleg is bearded-dragon body language. It may be the lizard's way of signaling that it's not interested in being top dragon.

This alligator is performing a head slap-jaw clap—a quick motion in which it snaps its jaws shut while smacking the water with the underside of its head. The sharp noise and splash may be a gator's way of loudly announcing, "It's me! I'm here!" Lots of tail thrashing is added for emphasis.

MAKING SENSE OF REPTILE SENSES

Sight, sound, smell, taste, and touch—the same senses you use are also employed by many reptiles. That's not to say they sense the world exactly as you do!

In Sight: Vision, for example, varies by species. Most lizards have very good eyesight for detecting both prey and predators. Chameleons, which shoot out their long tongues to catch prey, have eyes on turrets that can rotate independently and help them gauge distance. But amphisbaenians, which live underground, have scaled-over eyes that appear to sense only darkness and light; they don't need sharp eyesight in their world.

Hear This! Lizards differ from snakes when it comes to hearing. Most lizards have ear openings on the sides of their heads, but snakes do not. A snake does have an inner ear—the portion of the ear that's inside an animal's head. In snakes, however, the inner ear is connected to the jawbones instead of an eardrum. The snake's jaw picks up vibrations from the ground, so it can "hear" a tasty mouse scampering past, for example.

Recently, scientists have found evidence that snakes can also sense very loud airborne sounds because such sounds send vibrations into their bones. Amphisbaenians, turtles, and the tuatara also can hear.

Smell, Taste, and Touch! Snakes and lizards not only smell with their noses, but can also detect scents with their tongues. The tongue flicks out to gather particles from objects, the ground, and the air. Almost all reptiles, except for snakes, also have taste buds on their tongues.

Some snakes, such as pit vipers, some boas, and certain pythons (like this Burmese python), have heat-sensitive pits on their faces for detecting prey. They can "see" the heat of a mouse that's nearly a yard (1 m) away in pitch darkness.

Sea turtles can sense magnetic fields—a useful ability for navigating across a vast ocean! They share this ability with their distant relatives, birds.

A snake's tongue picks up particles from objects, the ground, and the air. Back inside the mouth, the particles are detected by a patch of cells called the Jacobson's organ. This organ helps a snake make quick choices about food, mates, and danger. Lizards have this organ, too.

A lizard doesn't have an outer ear that sticks out like your ear. What you can see on some reptiles' heads is an eardrum, or tympanic membrane. It appears as a flat or sunken disc on the skin. Many lizards have an ear opening that looks like a hole.

REPTILE COURTSHIP AND MATING

A little green lizard perches on a branch. He bobs his head and flares a pink flap of skin under his chin. Over and over, he performs this display. What's he doing?

The lizard, a green anole, is trying to attract a female anole. This kind of activity is called courtship behavior. Reptiles display a wide variety of courtship behaviors, all with the goal of mating to produce a new generation of their species.

Many other lizards also court females with behaviors like head bobbing and color changing. Many turtles and tortoises bob their heads, too. The males of some species of Asian river turtles add flashy breeding colors to their wardrobe: The male Asian river terrapin, for example, develops a black head and neck with a collar of bright orange-red during mating season, while the female remains a dull olive green.

Snakes are loners most of the time, but males seek out female snakes during mating season. At this time, if a male snake meets another male of his species, the two may fight. They wrestle with each other until one gives up. Male crocodylians also do battle. Meanwhile, males and females court each other. Depending on the species, courtship may involve swimming in circles, rubbing snouts, or blowing bubbles underwater!

Green sea turtles usually swim alone, but they gather in huge crowds to find mates during breeding season. Males and females seem to dance as they swim in circles around each other.

A tussle between two male snakes is called a combat dance. It involves a lot of shoving, struggling, and wrestling, but usually nobody gets hurt. This behavior is often mistaken for courtship behavior between a male and female because it's so dramatic.

A male American alligator makes water "sizzle" above his back to attract females! He does this by making very deep, low sounds. Some of these sounds travel underwater and can't be heard above the surface. But they make the alligator's body vibrate strongly, which causes water on his back to jump and bounce.

Side-blotched lizards live in dry lands and deserts of the western United States. Depending on throat color, males of this species have different "family lives": An orange-throated male guards a large territory. His mates are any females that wander onto his property. A blue-throated male guards his mates instead. He has a small territory but pairs up with just a few females, sometimes even just one. Yellow-throated males just sneak around and try to lure females away!

33

REPTILE REPRODUCTION

All birds lay eggs. Nearly all mammals give birth to live young.
But there is no one rule for reptiles. Many reptiles lay eggs like birds. Some reptiles give live birth to fully developed young, much like mammals do. Yet other reptiles bear young in a way that's like a blend of these two processes.

Most reptiles are "oviparous," which means they lay eggs that develop outside their bodies, like birds' eggs. The eggs have yolks inside them that provide the developing young, or embryos, with nutrients. Crocodylians and geckos lay eggs with hard shells, while other lizards, snakes, and amphisbaenians lay softer, leathery eggs. Tortoises and some turtles lay fairly hard-shelled eggs, but sea turtles and some freshwater turtles lay leathery eggs.

Oviparous reptiles lay their eggs in a safe place. Sea turtles, for example, dig holes in sand and bury their eggs. Alligators build a nest that is a compost heap of leaves, soil, and dirt. Many snakes and lizards lay eggs in leaf litter, soil, and other sheltered spots. Most reptiles provide no care for the eggs, but many crocodylians and some lizards and snakes do.

Some lizards and snakes, on the other hand, are "viviparous," which means they give birth to living young that don't develop inside an egg laid in a protected place. Instead, many of these reptiles keep their eggs inside their bodies so that the embryos develop and grow before the eggs are laid.

By the time these eggs leave the mother's body, the shells are just fragile, skinlike membranes around the hatchlings. The females lay these very soft eggs just as they're about to hatch so that their young are also born as completely developed little reptiles.

Some lizards' and snakes' bodies, however, provide their unborn young with nutrients instead of depending on yolks in the egg to do the job. This form of reproduction is similar to a mammal's, in which the young are nourished and sustained by the female's body up until birth.

A female American alligator builds a refrigerator-size nest of grass, sticks, leaves, and mud. She guards the nest until the eggs hatch. Many crocodylians guard their nests fiercely and dig them open when hatching time arrives.

A loggerhead sea turtle digs a nest for her eggs.

Most snakes leave their eggs after laying them. A few species, however, brood their eggs as birds do. Pythons, for example, curl around their eggs like a scaly scarf. Some pythons shiver to warm their eggs—shivering makes body heat that keeps the eggs cozy.

GROWING UP REPTILE

Whether they hatch from eggs or are live-born, most reptile young are on their own from the start. Some geckos, skinks, and other lizards defend their young, but most reptiles provide no care for their offspring. Young Komodo dragons even live in trees to stay out of reach of hungry adult dragons. The order Crocodylia, however, is filled with creatures that are so attentive to their young they would receive cards on Mother's Day and Father's Day, if reptiles could read!

The mugger crocodile of India, for example, guards its nest fiercely. When the young are ready to hatch, they chirp, and both the male and female muggers rush to dig up the nest. They even gather eggs in their mouth and gently press on them to help the babies hatch. Then they carry the tiny muggers to the water. The young crocs will be guarded for up to two years by their parents.

Reptile hatchlings often look like mini versions of adults. In some species, however, the youngsters may be different colors. Bright colors are common among lizard hatchlings. A young Dumeril's monitor lizard, for example, sports an orange head and black-and-yellow body.

Hatchlings, due to their small size, often eat different foods than their parents do. A newly hatched copperhead snake can't tackle the mice, big insects, and lizards that adults eat, so it goes after caterpillars and other small insects at first. Then it graduates to eating tiny frogs and lizards. A copperhead hatchling has a bright yellow tail, which it wiggles to lure its prey.

Like a baby bird, a baby reptile that hatches from an egg starts life with an "egg tooth" to help it open its shell. The egg tooth is a tough bump that is part of the skin on the snout or an actual extra tooth that sticks out of the mouth, depending on the species. The egg tooth is lost soon after hatching.

A python hatchling slices its way out of its leathery shell with the help of its pointed egg tooth. (Its mother, which curled around the eggs to protect them, leaves after they hatch.) The young snake must fend for itself as soon as it's out of its eggshell.

An American alligator mom carries her young in her mouth and ferries them to the water after hatching. A baby gator eats small prey such as spiders, insects, crabs, shrimp, and small fish.

It's a boy . . . or a girl? For many reptiles, it depends on temperature! In a variety of lizard and turtle species—and in all crocodylian species—the sex of hatchlings depends on how warm the eggs were during incubation. American alligator eggs kept at 93°F (34°C) and above all hatch as males, while eggs kept at 86°F (30°C) or below all hatch as females. The opposite is true for many turtles: Lower temperatures produce males, and higher temperatures produce females.

An ashy gecko hatchling starts life looking like a tiny tiger with a bright orange tail and a green-blue head. It changes to a speckly reddish brown as it grows. The adult and hatchling look so different that they were once thought to be two different species.

REPTILES ON THE MOVE

Walking, running, swimming, slithering, sliding, even gliding—reptiles have lots of ways of getting around!

The limbs of a four-legged lizard sprawl sideways instead of sticking straight down from its body as almost all land mammals' legs do. As a result, a lizard has to twist its body from side to side as it moves. But there is an advantage to this sprawled posture: When a reptile sits still, its body rests on the surface of whatever it's standing on, which saves energy—an important concern for an ectothermic animal. The downside is that a reptile's lungs can't work normally as its body twists while in motion. It has to stop to take a breath.

Crocodylians, however, are able to walk nearly upright on all fours. This is a stride called the "high walk." Turtles can lift their bodies off the ground, too.

Reptiles that swim may have feet adapted to propelling them through water. Turtles, for example, swim with their feet. Freshwater turtles typically have webbed feet that help push them through water. Sea turtles have flippers.

Many water-dwelling reptiles use their tails to swim. Crocodylians, for example, sweep their long, strong tails from side to side to propel themselves through the water. Their tails are flattened from top to bottom, which makes them work like oars.

Snakes lack legs, but that doesn't stop them from zipping around. A snake moves by wriggling from side to side, pushing against the ground and various objects as it crawls. It can also hitch along by moving first the front, then the back, of its body, like an accordion on the go. In addition, many snakes can travel in a straight line using their muscles and belly scales. The muscles move sections of the snake's underside forward, causing its belly scales to hook onto the surface under itself and pull it forward.

It's a bird! It's a plane! It's . . . a flying lizard? Yes! The flying dragon is a reptile that has evolved flaps of skin on its sides that allow it to glide through the treetops. To "fly," it stretches out its ribs to spread the flaps of skin like wings. It can glide 30 feet (9 m) and sometimes more.

A sea snake ripples through the water with the help of a paddle-like tail. A sea snake is helpless if it's washed up on shore, because its flattened body tips over on its side.

A painted turtle swims in freshwater ponds and lakes. It has webbed feet like a duck's that help it paddle. A turtle that stays on land, such as a gopher tortoise, has rounded, stumpy feet instead of webbed ones.

Some snakes that live in hot, sandy deserts have evolved a motion called sidewinding. A sidewinding snake throws its head and neck sideways, then sets it down. Leaving its tail in place, it lifts its middle and shifts it sideways, too. Then the tail starts to follow while the head and neck start moving again. Moving in this way, the snake never has its whole body pressed against the hot surface at the same time. It's also an efficient way to travel on shifting sand.

The basilisk lizard lives in trees near water. When it's threatened by a predator, it drops into the water and runs away across its surface.

HIDE-AND-SEEK: REPTILE CAMOUFLAGE

Motion can help a reptile survive—but so can sitting still! Many reptiles rely on their colors and patterns to help them hide in plain sight. A snake clad in brown and tan splotches disappears in a bed of leaves, a gray lizard vanishes among rocks. But some reptiles go way beyond camouflaging colors. They have body shapes and behaviors that also conceal them, helping them hide from predators and sneak up on prey.

Some reptiles, for example, resemble objects in their environment. The twig snake, as its name suggests, looks like a long, skinny twig. The lined leaf-tailed gecko, with its lean brown body, blends in with tree bark when it perches on a trunk. Alligators and crocodiles look like floating logs—until they lunge and chomp down on their prey.

The satanic leaf-tailed gecko is a superstar in the camouflage department. Its body and tail are both flattened and shaped like leaves. Nicks in the edges of the tail make it look as if it got nibbled.

The green vine snake winds through branches in rain forests of Central and northern South America. Looking like a vine helps the snake avoid detection as it sneaks up on prey. Even its tongue is long and green!

The blotch-tailed earless dragon lives in dry lands in central and western Australia. Its stumpy body and patchy, reddish color make it disappear among rocks. You can see why many people call it "pebble dragon"!

The Kenyan pygmy chameleon looks like a tiny stick. The bumpy scales on its face even give it the jagged edge of a broken twig. It's just the right disguise for a reptile that lurks in bushes.

SELF-DEFENSE

Freezing in place and relying on camouflage is one form of self-defense. So is leaving the scene and hiding. Approach a pond, for example, and you may hear plop, plop, plop as turtles slide off a log and into the water. These strategies are the first line of defense for many reptiles.

Other reptiles also have armor for protection from predators. A box turtle, for example, pulls its head, legs, and tail into its sturdy shell, which it can clamp shut. An Australian thorny devil lizard is covered with spikes.

Many reptiles attempt to look bigger than they really are and thus more threatening. A hog-nosed snake, for example, puffs up with air, flattens its neck so it looks wider, and hisses. If this doesn't scare off a predator, it tries a different trick: playing dead. It flops on its back, lolls out its tongue, and goes limp. This trick works because many predators won't eat animals they haven't killed themselves.

Some reptiles also warn predators not to mess with them. Sometimes, this warning is a bluff. A tiny horned wood lizard, for example, opens its brightly colored mouth to mean "stay away!" but its only real defense is nipping. Another warning that indicates a serious threat is when a rattlesnake shakes its tail. A rattlesnake's bite is not only painful—it also delivers a dose of a liquid toxin called venom.

Other reptiles flaunt warning coloration. The eastern coral snake, for example, is boldly patterned in red, yellow, and black stripes. These warning colors announce that the snake is venomous. Nonvenomous snakes such as milk snakes wear these colors, too. They gain protection by being copycats.

Some reptiles, like this rubber boa, use their tails in a way that makes them look as if they have two heads. This tactic can trick a predator into attacking the reptile's tail instead of its head. As a result, the reptile may escape with just a damaged tail instead of losing its all-important head. Sometimes, two heads are better than one!

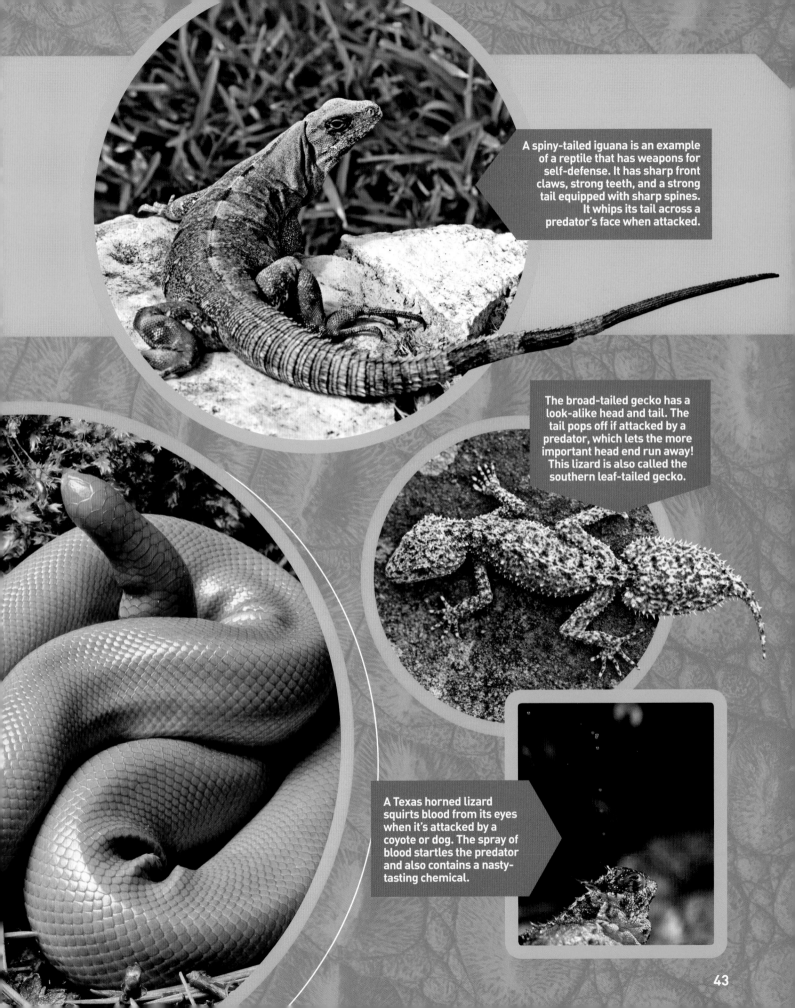

A spiny-tailed iguana is an example of a reptile that has weapons for self-defense. It has sharp front claws, strong teeth, and a strong tail equipped with sharp spines. It whips its tail across a predator's face when attacked.

The broad-tailed gecko has a look-alike head and tail. The tail pops off if attacked by a predator, which lets the more important head end run away! This lizard is also called the southern leaf-tailed gecko.

A Texas horned lizard squirts blood from its eyes when it's attacked by a coyote or dog. The spray of blood startles the predator and also contains a nasty-tasting chemical.

HABITATS: REPTILES AT HOME

From warm, wet rain forests to bone-dry deserts, reptiles have made themselves at home in nearly every habitat on Earth.
The only places you won't find them are in Antarctica or on the frozen peaks of very high mountains. These places are just too cold for a "cold-blooded" animal to survive.

Tropical habitats boast the largest variety of reptile species. Rain forests contain reptiles ranging from tiny lizards small enough to sit on a dime to giant snakes nearly as long as a school bus. Snakes, lizards, and tortoises thrive in hot deserts worldwide. The oceans teem with sea snakes and sea turtles. Lakes, rivers, marshes, and swamps support turtles, crocodylians, snakes, and lizards. Islands are populated by unusual reptiles such as the burly Komodo dragon.

Even cities are reptile habitats. The common house gecko of Southeast Asia, for example, is named for its habit of living in people's homes. In Bangkok, Thailand, reticulated pythons and water monitor lizards roam city parks. Italian wall lizards, native to dry, rocky places in the Mediterranean, are equally at home hanging out on walls, bridges, and other structures in cities. They're so frequently found on the remains of ancient buildings, they're also called "ruin lizards."

Hot-spring snakes of Tibet are slender snakes that live near hot springs and in fields at altitudes as high as 14,000 feet (4,270 m) and above in the Himalaya. There they feed on frogs and fish.

Remote islands are habitats where animals tend to be either much larger or much smaller than related species on the mainland. On the Galápagos Islands, for example, giant tortoises may have had a better chance at survival because they could survive longer without food or fresh water than smaller tortoises. A Galápagos tortoise can go for an entire year without eating or drinking!

Alligators live in wetlands and waterways. They use their feet and snouts to dig up dirt and plants to make their own small ponds called alligator holes. Other animals visit the holes to drink, especially during dry seasons when other water sources have dried up.

The desert horned viper lives in the Sahara, a desert in Africa. Its speckled coloring blends in with the sand. As if this camouflage isn't enough, the viper also shuffles its body until it's covered with sand and lies in wait for prey to wander into striking distance.

WINTER SLEEP, SUMMER SNOOZE

One habitat that's ideal for reptiles is the tropics. Tropical places have a steady, warm temperature and lots of moisture all year long. Reptiles in other habitats, however, have to endure seasonal changes in weather. How do these ectotherms survive in places with cold winters where temperatures plunge below freezing?

They do what some mammals do: ride out the season by taking shelter and becoming inactive. This process is called hibernating. It's often called brumating by reptile experts, because it differs in some ways from mammal hibernation. A reptile, after all, is used to its temperature dropping significantly and its body functions slowing down when it's cold. A mammal is not.

A reptile stops eating before it gets ready to hibernate. Then it seeks out a sheltered place. Lizards such as the five-lined skink hibernate beneath rocks, in rotting logs, or under piles of leaves. Rattlesnakes gather by the dozens in shared dens. Box turtles dig burrows. Water-dwelling turtles tuck themselves into mud at the bottom of a pond or lake.

During hibernation, reptiles do not eat or produce waste. Their body functions, including heart and breathing rates, slow down. Hibernating water turtles can even get all the oxygen they need by absorbing it directly from the water through special areas in the skin, the throat, and the hind end, instead of breathing with the lungs.

Reptiles can also survive extremely hot, dry conditions by estivating—that's the "avoid the heat" form of hibernating. They hole up in a cool burrow or other spot and go dormant until the drought is over.

Japanese five-lined skinks can survive the cold winter months by hibernating in underground burrows.

In some places, reptiles hibernate in large groups. These shared dens are called hibernacula. Garter snake species throughout the United States gather in hibernacula and then emerge again in the spring.

The thorny devil lives in the Australian desert. It avoids the hottest days by staying inside a shallow burrow. But it still gets thirsty. No water? No problem! The thorny devil's body is covered with fine grooves that channel water to its mouth. Thanks to these grooves, it can even drink water droplets that collect on its body on a chilly night.

The dinner-plate turtle of Australia lives in rivers that form during rainy seasons. When the rivers dry up, the turtle estivates, burying itself in a burrow. Its body gets all the water it needs to survive from a supply stored up in its bladder. The turtle can live for two years in this state.

FROM ANTS TO ZEBRAS:
WHAT REPTILES EAT

Food is one of the most important features of a reptile's habitat. The menu at a restaurant for reptiles would be enormous. It would have to include everything from insect eggs and algae to flowers, rats . . . and other reptiles.

Many lizard species feed mainly on insects and other invertebrates, such as worms, ants, termites, spiders, slugs, snails, and scorpions. Amphisbaenians gobble up worms, insects, and larvae. Various snakes eat small invertebrates, too. Blind snakes survive on them, consuming mainly ants and termites. Shieldtail snakes eat worms. Keeled slug-eating snakes gulp down huge numbers of slugs (and guess what the snail-eating snake eats?). The young of many snakes also eat insects, as do crocodylian hatchlings.

Vertebrates are also important prey for many reptiles. Snakes of many species consume rats, mice, and other rodents. Other snakes go after frogs, fish, reptiles, or birds. The biggest ones, such as pythons, eat antelope, goats, and other large mammals. Crocodylians eat all these animals, too, with the largest species taking down prey such as deer, zebras, and water buffalo. Reptiles that eat other reptiles include king snakes, which prey on other snakes. Snakes will also eat lizards. Big lizards eat smaller lizards.

Plants form some or all of various reptiles' diets. Many turtles are omnivores—animals that eat both plants and animals. The wood turtle, for example, dines on fungi as well as on worms. Marine iguanas are strictly plant-eaters, or herbivores: They graze on seaweed, scraping it off rocks with their teeth.

Some reptiles actively hunt prey, while others ambush it. This sit-and-wait strategy works for chameleons. A chameleon stands stock-still, moving only its eyes to zero in on its target. Then it shoots out its tongue, which stretches longer than its body length in barely one-sixteenth of a second. The sticky end of the tongue seizes the prey and reels it into its mouth.

What a crocodylian eats depends partly on where it lives but also on its size. A small croc called the Cuvier's dwarf caiman eats rodents and fish as well as shrimp and crabs. The biggest croc species, the saltwater crocodile, can devour large mammals. But like all crocs, it will eagerly snap up little fish and other small "snacks" that cross its path.

Egg-eating snakes live in parts of Africa and India. Special teeth and spines in their throats crush eggshells and squeeze out the egg contents.

The green sea turtle is a herbivore as an adult. It eats algae and sea grasses. Baby green sea turtles, however, mostly eat crabs and other invertebrates.

REPTILES AS PREY

Just as reptiles eat other animals, so too do many animals prey on reptiles. Little reptiles are eaten by predators ranging from spiders and praying mantises to birds and coyotes. Bigger reptiles face fewer predators, though they're just as vulnerable as the little guys when they're young.

Small lizards are snapped up by predators in every habitat. They're favorite meals for birds such as roadrunners and shrikes. Shrikes often save food for later by impaling it on thorns, and many unfortunate lizards end up as tree "decorations" in this way! Snakes and other lizards also make meals of small lizards.

Snakes, too, are feasted on by birds. Snake eagles, as you might guess, specialize in eating snakes. These birds of prey live in parts of Africa and Asia. Extra-thick scales on their legs protect them from snakebites. The birds start eating their prey headfirst even while in flight!

Amphisbaenians are safe from many predators because they live underground. Most of them also have a strong bite. Some snakes, however, are able to subdue them. These snakes tend to have strong skulls and jaws or a venomous bite. Other animals eat amphisbaenians when they find them on the ground instead of under it.

Turtles are well protected by their shells, but for some predators the shell is nothing more than packaging. Sea turtles, for example, are eaten by sharks and orcas. Bearded vultures drop tortoises onto rocks to break their shells. Crocodiles and alligators easily crunch up turtles. Mammalian predators such as jaguars can sometimes defeat a turtle's armor, too.

Likewise, crocodylian eggs and hatchlings feed a variety of animals, but far fewer creatures prey on the adults. Smaller crocs, such as caimans, are caught by big predators such as jaguars and pythons, but the biggest species, as adults, are preyed on mainly by humans. Humans are also the main predators of adult turtles, both large and small.

Some reptiles are so tiny, they fall prey to insects, spiders, and other invertebrates. Large insects like mantises can seize small lizards just as they seize other insects. Small lizards can even get stuck in spiderwebs.

Sometimes reptiles are their own worst enemies! Snapping turtles eat snakes. Many snakes eat lizards, and some eat other snakes. Giant snakes, such as the anaconda of South America, can kill caimans. In Australia, pythons have even eaten crocodiles. Crocodiles, in turn, have also eaten pythons.

Turtle eggs are a feast for many animals, such as this raccoon. Raccoons also raid the nests of American alligators, as do skunks, opossums, bears, and pigs. Ants, skunks, badgers, and snakes all eat lizard eggs.

The roadrunner is a fast-running bird of the southwestern United States. It eats lizards, small rodents, and snakes— even venomous rattlesnakes! The bird attacks a rattlesnake by seizing its head and bashing it repeatedly on a rock.

51

MAKING A FUTURE FOR REPTILES:
CONSERVATION AT WORK

Reptiles have existed for millions of years. The fossil record shows that many species have barely changed in all that time. Yet today, about one out of five reptile species is threatened with extinction. Unlike dinosaurs, which were wiped out by a natural disaster, modern reptiles' problems are caused by human activity.

In some countries, for example, reptiles are heavily hunted for food and skins and, sadly, for body parts to be used as souvenirs and trinkets. Reptiles' body parts are also used to make ingredients for "folk medicines" that people think will heal them. And reptiles are caught and sold as pets, often illegally.

Loss of habitat also harms reptiles. When an area is cleared to build structures such as shopping centers, reptiles are forced out. Fires and pollution can also destroy habitats.

The blue iguana of Grand Cayman island in the Caribbean came close to extinction. People brought cats and dogs to the island, which killed iguana hatchlings. Habitat destruction hurt iguanas, as well. By 2002, only 10 to 25 blue iguanas survived in the wild. Today, thanks to conservation efforts that include hatching iguanas in captivity and releasing them as adults, about 800 blue iguanas live in the wild in protected areas.

Lake Erie water snakes live on islands in North America's Lake Erie. Their numbers dropped as buildings were constructed in their habitat. The species was declared threatened in 1999. After an education campaign to teach people about snakes, as well as habitat protection, the snake's numbers increased so much that it was taken off the list of threatened species in 2011.

Here, a Philippine crocodile is being measured at the London Zoo. The Philippine crocodile became endangered as wetlands in the Philippines were turned into rice paddies. Hunting also reduced its numbers. Today, organizations worldwide are working with farmers and the Philippine government to protect crocs and their habitat. Safe places, called sanctuaries, have been created for the reptiles. These sanctuaries conserve wetlands for other animals, too. Today, about 250 of these rare crocs live in the wild.

Sea turtles accidentally caught in shrimp nets often drown. Today, shrimp boats are often equipped with "turtle excluder devices," or TEDs, which have metal bars that stop sea turtles from entering the part of the net that holds the shrimp catch. Then the turtles can escape through a special gap in the net. Thanks to TEDs, about 97 percent of captured turtles escape successfully.

Invasive species—animals that aren't natural to a habitat—are a major threat, too. Rats, for example, eat reptile eggs as well as small reptiles. Rats and other introduced mammals caused many island reptiles, such as the tuatara of New Zealand, to become endangered.

Fortunately, many people are working to save reptiles and their habitats. They are educating people so they'll understand that reptiles aren't creepy, evil creatures—they're fascinating animals that also play important roles in their environments. Many reptiles, for example, are food for other wild animals that would go hungry without them. Reptiles that eat mice, rats, and insects that damage crops help keep down the numbers of these animals.

Plans and projects that prevent extinction are part of a bigger effort called wildlife conservation. Conserving animals means protecting them and their habitats so they can survive, and using resources such as water wisely so that we don't harm our environment.

One example of successful reptile-conservation efforts is the use of "turtle excluder devices," or TEDs, on shrimp boats. (See photo caption below left for details.) Other success stories include rat-eradication projects on islands. In the late 1980s, for example, an extermination program killed off the invasive rats that preyed on the native wildlife of New Zealand's Korapuki Island. Populations of endangered skinks began to rise after the rats were gone.

By conserving reptiles and their habitats, we make the world a better place for all living things—including humans!

LIZARDS, SNAKES, & WORM LIZARDS

ALL ABOUT LIZARDS

Lizards, along with snakes and amphisbaenians, form the reptile group known as squamates. Lizards have by far the most number of species. There are nearly 6,000 species of lizards, more than there are species of mammals, and new ones are being discovered all the time.

Like birds, lizards boast a wide variety of colors, patterns, and forms. They range in size from tiny creatures that can fit in a teaspoon, such as the Jaragua lizard of the West Indies, to the biggest lizard of all, the mighty Komodo dragon of Indonesia, which is large enough to kill a buffalo.

Lizards are most plentiful and diverse in tropical places, but they are able to live in a variety of habitats and temperature ranges. There is even a lizard species that lives north of the Arctic Circle!

Lizards have scales of different sizes, and most species have eyelids that can move and visible external ears. Most have four legs, though some species have reduced legs or none at all. Their skulls and jaws are flexible so the mouth can open wide.

An important difference between lizards and snakes lies inside them: Lizards, like you and most other animals with backbones, are symmetrical inside. That means most of their organs come in pairs, and the right side looks a lot like the left. A lizard, for example, has two lungs side by side. A snake, however, has one long right lung and a tiny left lung (or no left lung at all!), and other organs have to sit one behind the other so they can fit in its long, narrow body.

Like all reptiles, lizards have a cloaca—a single opening in their tail end that is shared by the urinary system, the digestive system, and the reproductive system.

Australian red-tailed skink
(Morethia storri)
This fire-tailed skink of northern Australia was declared a newly discovered species in 1980.

Green forest lizard
(Calotes calotes)
A male green forest lizard's orange head gets brighter during the breeding season.

Labord's chameleon
(Furcifer labordi)
A Labord's chameleon spends about nine months as an egg and then lives for only four to five months after hatching.

Banded galliwasp
(Diploglossus fasciatus)
A young banded galliwasp sits on a leaf in a forest in Brazil.

Blue-tailed day gecko
(Phelsuma cepediana)
The blue-tailed day gecko lives on the island of Mauritius, where it's an important pollinator for a rare plant.

Giant horned lizard
(Phrynosoma asio)
The giant horned lizard of Mexico is 6 to 8 inches (15–20 cm) long, making it the largest species of horned lizard.

LEOPARD GECKO

FAMILY
Gekkonidae

FACTS

OTHER COMMON NAMES
Spotted fat-tailed gecko, common leopard gecko

SCIENTIFIC NAME
Eublepharis macularius

SIZE
7–9 inches (18–23 cm)

FOOD
Insects, spiders, scorpions, other lizards, snails, bird eggs, fruit

HABITAT
Rocky deserts, dry grasslands

RANGE
Asia, Middle East

Lots of spots dot a leopard gecko, a pattern that gives the species its name. The spots help camouflage this ground-dwelling lizard among dirt and pebbles in its hot, dry habitat. The gecko avoids the heat by spending the day in a cool burrow or under a rock, coming out at sunset to hunt in the cool of night.

Like many lizards, a leopard gecko stores fat in its tail. The tail's size and shape make it look like the gecko's head. This similarity protects the gecko by tricking a predator into attacking the tail instead of the head. A vertebra in the tail then snaps along built-in fracture lines, which causes the tail to break away from the body. The predator is distracted by the loose, wriggling tail while the rest of the gecko runs away to live another day!

This deliberate tail loss is called caudal autotomy. Tail loss is a common strategy among lizards. There is little blood loss because the tail's muscles constrict and its blood vessels quickly shrink to shut off the blood flow in the injured area. A new tail starts growing right away. In about two months' time, the gecko has a new tail— shorter and plumper than the original one, but a tail nonetheless.

Many geckos lack movable eyelids. Their eyes are covered by clear, fused eyelids—a structure called a spectacle or brille. A leopard gecko, however, has movable eyelids. It can blink and close its eyes when it naps.

A young, or juvenile, leopard gecko is brightly colored with dark bands instead of spots. The bands fade as it grows.

The sticking force created by setae is so strong, a gecko can hang on with just one of its toes! Yet its feet easily peel off the surface when it wants to move, and its toes don't stick to each other.

The tokay gecko, like many geckos, doesn't have movable eyelids. Its eyes are covered with clear scales instead. The gecko often licks these scales to keep them clean, using its tongue as a windshield wiper!

TOKAY GECKO

The tokay gecko is one of the world's largest gecko species. The male is a little bigger than the female and also more brightly colored. He's also very noisy! A male calls "TO-KAY!" loudly during the breeding season to attract a mate. As you might guess, that's how the tokay gecko got its name. Even the word "gecko" is an imitation of a gecko's call.

A female gecko lays one or two eggs in a protected spot, such as in a rock crevice or under tree bark. The eggs stick to the surface and harden in place. Both the male and female guard the eggs until they hatch. Tokay geckos have managed to travel to other countries as eggs because females sometimes lay them on objects such as crates that are later loaded onto ships. The hatchlings can survive in their new habitat if it offers living conditions like those in their homeland.

Like other climbing geckos, a tokay gecko has broad toes on its feet. Each toe is lined with ridges, which are covered by hundreds of thousands of extremely small "hairs" called setae. Each seta is fringed, like a tiny broom, with hundreds of bristles.

The molecules of the bristles' flat tips are attracted to molecules in a surface due to a weak electrical force. This weak bond is very strong when it's shared by billions of bristles—strong enough to let a gecko stick to a surface, even a very smooth one, such as glass.

FAMILY
Gekkonidae

FACTS

OTHER COMMON NAMES
Common gecko

SCIENTIFIC NAME
Gekko gecko

SIZE
7–14 inches (18–36 cm)

FOOD
Insects, scorpions, lizards; small snakes, birds, and mammals

HABITAT
Rain forests

RANGE
Southeast Asia

NAMIB WEB-FOOTED GECKO

FAMILY
Gekkonidae

FACTS

OTHER COMMON NAMES
Palmatogecko, Namib desert gecko, Namib sand gecko, web-footed gecko

SCIENTIFIC NAME
Pachydactylus rangei

SIZE
4–6 inches (10–15 cm)

FOOD
Insects, spiders

HABITAT
Desert

RANGE
Southwest Africa

The Namib web-footed gecko is named in part after where it lives: the Namib Desert of southern Africa. The Namib is a very dry desert. Some parts of it receive less than 0.2 inches (5 mm) of rain in a year. Most of the water that sustains life in the desert comes from fog that blows in from the desert's western edge, which is bordered by the Atlantic Ocean.

The web-footed gecko is adapted to life in this dry land. Its mottled pink-brown skin camouflages it in the sand. It has webbed feet, with stiff fibers and muscles running through the webbing. The feet work like snowshoes to help the gecko walk on shifting sand.

At night, the web-footed gecko emerges to hunt insects, relying on its supersize eyes to find them. During the cool hours of night, mist and fog condense on the gecko's body. Every time the gecko licks these dewdrops off the clear spectacles on its eyes, it gets a drink of water! The rest of the water it needs comes mainly from its juicy prey.

The Namib web-footed gecko can bend its feet into scoops and use them to dig a burrow in the sand. It stays inside the burrow by day to avoid the heat.

A female web-footed gecko lays two eggs about the size of beans. She buries them in sand, where their sticky shells quickly harden.

A Kuhl's flying gecko appears on an Indian coin that was minted in 2011. It featured wildlife of the Andaman and Nicobar Islands, a territory that is part of India.

The Kuhl's flying gecko is widespread in Southeast Asia. Its tail, feet, and coloring differ from place to place. Some scientists suggest some of these different geckos may really be different species.

KUHL'S FLYING GECKO

At rest, a Kuhl's flying gecko clings to a tree.

It presses its body tightly against the trunk. Flaps of skin on its sides, legs, tail, and head spread around it. These flaps help blur its lizard-body shape and make it harder for a predator to see it. Its gray-brown color and blotchy markings camouflage it, too.

But it's impossible to miss this gecko when it suddenly drops from the tree and takes to the air! It stretches out its legs and tail so that its flaps open wide. It spreads its webbed toes, too. Then the gecko dives as if it's wearing a parachute. It can also glide for short distances. Finally, it swoops upward just before landing on a new tree trunk.

Parachuting and gliding enable the gecko to escape predators and travel to new trees to look for food. Kuhl's flying gecko is one of several kinds of parachute geckos that live in the dense rain forests of Southeast Asia, which are also home to flying mammals, frogs, and even snakes!

FAMILY
Gekkonidae

FACTS

OTHER COMMON NAMES
Gliding gecko, Kuhl's parachute gecko

SCIENTIFIC NAME
Ptychozoon kuhli

SIZE
7–8 inches (18–20 cm)

FOOD
Insects

HABITAT
Rain forests

RANGE
Southeast Asia

BURTON'S SNAKE-LIZARD

When is a snake not a snake? When it's a snake-lizard! A snake-lizard is a kind of lizard that lacks front legs and has just tiny flaps in place of hind legs. Its unblinking eyes and long, skinny body make it look like a snake. Unlike a snake, though, it has visible ear holes in the sides of its head, and it doesn't have a deeply forked tongue.

Burton's snake-lizard belongs to a group of reptiles called flap-footed lizards. Most flap-footed lizards eat insects, but Burton's snake-lizard preys on other lizards and sometimes snacks on snakes. Its skull and jaws are very flexible, which enables it to close its jaws around its prey so that the tips of its jaws meet in front. This ability gives it a good grip on a smooth, scaly reptile. Its teeth are also hinged so that they fold back to let prey slide in easily, but lock in place to snag the prey if it tries to wriggle back out. Its strong tongue forces the prey into position so that it's swallowed headfirst.

The snake-lizard hides from hawks and other predators by hunkering down in leaf litter. If it's attacked, it slithers quickly away—and if it needs more speed, it uses its tail to help it leap forward.

The snake-lizard hunts by lying quietly, then lunging when prey comes near. Its long, pointed snout helps it grab its victim quickly. Its muscular tongue and ear holes are clues that tell you this animal isn't a snake.

The hind legs of a legless lizard are just little scaly flaps. They give these animals their name of "flap-footed lizards." They also inspired the scientific family name Pygopodidae, which means "rump-footed."

Not all green iguanas are green. In Peru, they are often green-blue with blue and black markings. In Central America, green iguanas may be tinted with red and orange.

In breeding season, a male green iguana turns orange. He can often be seen bobbing his head on a highly visible spot, such as a dead tree, to show off for females.

GREEN IGUANA

Dragonlike green iguanas lurk in rain forest treetops throughout Central and South America and the Caribbean. Unlike storybook dragons, however, iguanas aren't predators. These big lizards, like other iguanas, are herbivores—animals that eat plants. (Hatchlings, however, eat insects.)

Unlike most lizards, iguanas are social creatures. They're often seen basking in groups in trees near water. When threatened by a predator, an iguana escapes by jumping into the water and swimming away, paddling with its long, strong tail. Iguanas have also been observed falling 40 feet (12 m) onto solid ground, then running away uninjured. If caught, however, this big lizard is far from helpless. It has raking claws, razor-sharp teeth, and a whiplash tail.

Some people keep iguanas as pets, though they are difficult to care for and should be kept only by those with lots of experience in handling reptiles. Unfortunately, some thoughtless people, who realize too late that iguanas require special handling, get rid of them by releasing them in the wild. As a result, iguanas have established themselves in parts of Florida and Hawaii in the United States, and in other warm places. In Central and South America, iguanas are often dinner instead of pets! They're sometimes referred to as "the chickens of the trees."

FAMILY
Iguanidae

FACTS

OTHER COMMON NAMES
Common iguana

SCIENTIFIC NAME
Iguana iguana

SIZE
5–6.5 feet (1.5–2 m)

FOOD
Fruit, flowers, leaves

HABITAT
Forests near a water source

RANGE
Mexico to South America; Caribbean; Florida and Hawaii

GALÁPAGOS MARINE IGUANA

"Disgusting, clumsy lizards!" That's how British scientist Charles Darwin described marine iguanas when he first saw them while exploring the Galápagos Islands in 1835. But "amazingly unique lizards" would be a better description of this one-of-a-kind reptile, the only lizard in the world that swims and feeds in the ocean.

A marine iguana's dark gray or black skin helps it absorb the sun's warmth as it basks before plunging into the cold sea. It swims by waving its flattened tail from side to side. While underwater, it feeds on seaweed that grows on rocks by scraping it off with sharp teeth. After it emerges, it will climb back on the dark lava rocks so it can warm up again, clinging to them with its sharp, curved claws. At night, when the air is cold, marine iguanas huddle in heaps to sleep.

During the mating season, males on different islands may change color, turning shades of red, green, or both. They court females by creeping up to them and bobbing their heads. A month later, it's the females' turn to bob their heads at each other as they compete for nesting sites in the sand. In this case, head-bobbing means "stay away." After laying eggs, a female guards her nest for several days. When the eggs hatch a few months later, the juveniles are on their own. They eat seaweed found on the rocky shore when the tide goes out.

The ocean is salty, so a marine iguana consumes a lot of salt in its diet of seaweed. This salt builds up in its blood. Glands in the iguana's nose filter out excess salt, which is then expelled by sneezing. Any salty spray that lands on the iguana's head dries up to form a white helmet!

A marine iguana shrinks when food is scarce! Researchers noticed that when the seaweed supply ran low for two years due to changes in ocean currents, the iguanas got shorter in length. Smaller iguanas need less food, so shrinking helped them survive. They grew again when food was plentiful.

Young chuckwallas have banded bodies and boldly striped tails. Adult females have fainter bands. Males typically have black heads and forelegs, and their middles are often orange or red.

The name "chuckwalla" is based on a Native American word for this lizard. Native Americans hunted chuckwallas for food. Chuckwallas also appear in Native American stories and artwork.

CHUCK-WALLA

The hefty chuckwalla's life is centered on rocks.
It basks on rocks. It seeks shade among rocks. In winter, it
hibernates among rocks. If danger threatens, it dives into a crevice
among rocks. Then the chuckwalla turns itself into a reptile balloon!
It forces extra air into its lungs by pulsing its cheeks and throat,
taking in four times as much air as it usually does. The inflated
lungs puff up its body so that it becomes firmly wedged in place.
No amount of pulling will enable a predator to yank it out.

This habit explains the saggy, baggy skin of a chuckwalla—it
wears size extra-large so that it has room to expand. Its skin is also
covered with rough scales that snag on the rocks. The lizard hangs on
with its strong claws.

The chuckwalla is the second largest lizard in the United States;
only the Gila monster is larger (see pages 112–113). It feeds on flowers,
leaves, and fruit. Water is scarce in the desert, but a chuckwalla gets
the liquid it needs from its food. Its body also saves water by producing
waste that is very concentrated—more pasty,
like a bird's—rather than in liquid urine
form. This process can leave its blood
too salty, so the lizard gets rid of
extra salt through its nose.
That's why the chuckwalla
sometimes has white rings
around its nostrils!

FAMILY
Iguanidae

FACTS

OTHER COMMON NAMES
Chuckawalla, chuck, common
chuckwalla

SCIENTIFIC NAME
Sauromalus ater

SIZE
11–16.5 inches (28–42 cm)

FOOD
Leaves, fruit, flowers, buds

HABITAT
Open, rocky places;
deserts with rocky hills

RANGE
Western United States,
northern Mexico

GREEN ANOLE

FACTS

OTHER COMMON NAMES
American chameleon,
Carolina anole

SCIENTIFIC NAME
Anolis carolinensis

SIZE
5–8 inches (13–20 cm)

FOOD
Insects, spiders, small crabs

HABITAT
Woodlands, gardens, parks

RANGE
Southeastern United States

Fences, rooftops, walls, branches, and tree trunks—they're all good places for basking and hunting if you're an American green anole.

This common lizard of the southeastern United States is as much at home in parks and gardens as it is in swamps and woodlands.

Green anoles are good climbers and can even walk up a sheet of glass, like a gecko. They turn a bright emerald green when they bask in sunlight. They turn brown on a cool day or when they're in the shade. Anoles' moods can also cause color changes. An angry male anole will turn bright green when he challenges another male who steps onto his territory. He'll also flare his vivid pink dewlap, a flap of skin on his throat. A male also shows off the dewlap to attract a female.

The green anole is the only anole native to the United States. Other anole species live in the West Indies and Central and South America. Some of these non-native species pop up in parts of the United States, too. They have usually escaped or were released by their owners. Non-native species are often harmful to native species. The brown anole of Cuba, for example, arrived in the United States as a stowaway aboard ships in the late 1800s. It takes over green anoles' territory, eats their eggs, and competes with them for food.

Male anoles may change color multiple times when they fight. When the battle is over, the male who wins is brilliant green. The loser turns brown.

A male green anole displays his dewlap. Females have much smaller dewlaps. The colors and patterns of different species help anoles recognize others of the same kind.

Male collared lizards open their mouths wide to threaten each other. Bright patches in the mouth show off each lizard's strong jaw muscles. Usually one lizard backs off before a fight erupts.

A collared lizard can sprint at speeds up to 16 miles an hour (26 km/h). It may run this fast to escape a predator or to chase another male off his territory.

COMMON COLLARED LIZARD

The common collared lizard gets its name from the black-and-white collar around its neck. Male collared lizards are brightly attired in blue and green and spattered with spots. Their heads and feet may be yellow or orange. Females wear duller colors, but when they're carrying eggs, they're speckled with orange spots on their sides.

This lizard is active during the day, spending its time looking for food and basking on rocks. If a predator approaches, it runs away to hide among rocks. It can put on an extra burst of speed by running on just its hind legs, which are longer than its front ones. A collared lizard even jumps from rock to rock on its hind legs, like a reptilian kangaroo.

The common name "collared lizard" is also used for other *Crotaphytus* species, such as the Great Basin collared lizard of the western United States and the Sonoran collared lizard of Mexico and Arizona, U.S.A. Both of these lizards were once considered subspecies of the common collared lizard.

Collared lizards are known to be feisty: They don't hesitate to bite if they feel threatened. Their jaws are adapted for chomping down on other lizards, so their bite is quite strong!

FAMILY
Crotaphytidae

FACTS

OTHER COMMON NAMES
Eastern collared lizard, Oklahoma collared lizard, mountain boomer

SCIENTIFIC NAME
Crotaphytus collaris

SIZE
8–14 inches (20–36 cm)

FOOD
Insects, spiders, lizards, small snakes, flowers, berries, leaves

HABITAT
Forests, dry grasslands, desert scrublands, rocky hillsides

RANGE
Midwestern and western North America

SHORT-HORNED LIZARD

FAMILY
Phrynosomatidae

OTHER COMMON NAMES
Greater short-horned lizard, Hernandez's short-horned lizard, horned toad

SCIENTIFIC NAME
Phrynosoma hernandesi

SIZE
3.5–6 inches (9–15 cm)

FOOD
Mainly ants; also other insects, spiders, snails

HABITAT
Prairies, sagebrush deserts, woodlands, dry lands high on mountainsides

RANGE
Western North America from southern Canada into central Mexico

FACTS

With its spiky head and neck, a short-horned lizard looks a bit like a miniature triceratops. Its back, sides, and tail are covered with prickles, too. This armor makes a short-horned lizard a very unpleasant mouthful for a predator! That is, if the predator can even find the lizard, whose coloring provides perfect camouflage amid soil, sand, and stones. If detected, however, the short-horned lizard will run away.

The lizard has a few other tricks if it's cornered: It puffs up its body to twice its normal size, which makes it harder to catch and swallow. It also opens its mouth wide, hisses, and charges at its foe. Weirdest of all, it can spray jets of blood from the corners of its eyes! It uses this tactic against dogs, foxes, and coyotes. The blood appears to irritate the mouths of these animals. The lizards don't squirt blood at other predators, such as snakes and birds.

More than a dozen "horned toad" species live in North and Central America. They're all prickly, though only a few species can squirt blood. They feast on insects, mainly ants. A hungry short-horned lizard will often squat next to an ant trail and gobble up ants as they march past. It might eat more than 200 ants in one day.

A short-horned lizard can send a spray of blood flying from 3.5 to 6 inches (9–15 cm). The blood comes from small vessels that burst when blood pressure rises in the lizard's head.

Female short-horned lizards give birth to live young. Mom provides no care—the babies fend for themselves.

79

A variety of mammals, birds, fish, and reptiles deter predators by signaling "I see you." The yellow-headed gecko is an example of a lizard that waves its tail before fleeing.

The male zebra-tailed lizard is more brightly colored than the female and has two dark bars on his sides. In breeding season, blue patches appear on his sides, too.

ZEBRA-TAILED LIZARD

Zebra-tailed lizards zip across the desert at up to 17 miles an hour (27 km/h). Their speedy sprints aren't for chasing down prey; zebra-tails typically wait for insects to wander by and then pounce on them, and they'll also leap into the air to catch flying insects. Running is reserved for escaping their own predators, such as snakes, roadrunners, foxes, coyotes, and bigger lizards.

Before the lizard runs, however, it wags its wildly striped tail. It will also wag its tail whenever it pauses during its escape. The wagging is a signal to the predator that says, "I see you, I know you're stalking me, so you might as well give up because you can't sneak up on me now."

The zebra-tail is an early riser, out and about feeding in the morning before other lizards have emerged. On cool mornings, however, it sleeps late! The lizard waits until it's warm enough to bask in the sun. It copes well with desert heat, staying busy all day long, though it will hide under a bush during the hottest hours. When it's standing on hot sand, it curls up its toes and holds its tail in the air to cut down on how much of its body is touching the ground—a habit it shares with many other lizards, such as the ring-tailed dragon of Australia.

FAMILY
Phrynosomatidae

FACTS

OTHER COMMON NAMES
Zebra-tail lizard, *perrito* ("little dog")

SCIENTIFIC NAME
Callisaurus draconoides

SIZE
6–9 inches (15–23 cm)

FOOD
Insects, spiders, lizards; sometimes leaves, flowers, and fruit

HABITAT
Deserts, dry streambeds

RANGE
Southwestern United States, northern Mexico

TROPICAL THORNYTAIL IGUANA

Tropical thornytail lizards don't make life easy for herpetologists who study them! These lizards live high in the treetops of the Amazon rain forest. Some trees here may grow as tall as 200 feet (61 m). But thornytails don't live in just any old tree. They require trees with trunks and branches that have thick, uneven bark to hide under and holes in which to live.

Such a tree is a kingdom for a thornytail, and you can tell which lizard is king at just a glance. A male thornytail who's "in charge" of a tree develops an orange head and a black body. Females and young thornytails on the tree are brown with yellowish speckles. If any other adult male thornytails live there, they are clad in these same colors.

A male thornytail typically shares his tree with several females and a few youngsters. As many as 20 lizards may live in one tree. A female lays up to two eggs at a time in a deep tree hole. Researchers have found as many as 14 eggs in one nest, and they speculate that all the females in the tree may lay their eggs in the same hole.

Ants also nest in the treetops, and they're the favorite food of thornytails. Like horned toads and other ground-dwelling ant-eaters, the thornytail will often sit, wait for ants to wander by, and then gobble them up as they pass.

The function of a thornytail's wide, flat, spiky tail is unknown. Its shape may help soak up sunlight so the lizard warms up quickly or it may work to block up the entrance of a hiding spot.

The green thornytail iguana is the only other species in the genus *Uracentron*. It also eats ants, lives high in the trees of the Amazon rain forest, and boasts a prickly tail.

Basilisk lizards are named after a creature in Greek and Roman stories. This mythical basilisk was said to be able to kill other animals merely by looking at them or breathing on them.

The basilisk's foot slaps down hard on the water, shoving water out of the way. This lets a pocket of air form around the foot, which stops it from sinking. The foot rises quickly before the air pocket fills up again. The basilisk's trick works only at top speed.

PLUMED BASILISK

If you ask a friend to draw a dragon, you might get back a storybook creature that actually looks like a plumed basilisk. The male of this Central American rain forest species is decorated with a spiny fan that runs down its back and another fan on its tail. Yet another crest sits on its head. The female lacks these adornments.

The basilisk is one of the most famous lizard species because of its habit of running across water when it's fleeing danger, such as a hungry snake twining along its tree branch. When the basilisk detects a snake, it plunges out of the tree and into the water. As soon as it splashes down, it starts running. It raises its body, front legs, and tail and pedals madly with its hind legs. Its long tail helps it balance as it sprints across the water's surface.

This ability to run on water is possible thanks to the structure of the basilisk's toes. The toes are lined with fringes, which open wide as the foot smacks down on the water, making it expand to support the lizard. The lizard quickly lifts its foot before water rushes in to fill the air pocket above the foot. As the foot rises, the fringes fold up and lie flat, which streamlines the toes so they move quickly through the air.

A basilisk can run for about 15 feet (4.6 m) before it finally sinks, at which point it starts swimming.

FAMILY
Corytophanidae

FACTS

OTHER COMMON NAMES
Green basilisk, double-crested basilisk, Jesus Christ lizard

SCIENTIFIC NAME
Basiliscus plumifrons

SIZE
24–28 inches (60–70 cm)

FOOD
Insects, snails, fish, frogs, small lizards, fruit, flowers

HABITAT
Rain forests, near water

RANGE
Central America and northern South America

RAINBOW AGAMA

FACTS

OTHER COMMON NAMES
Rainbow lizard, red-headed rock
agama, red-headed agama,
house agama, common agama

SCIENTIFIC NAME
Agama agama

SIZE
9–12 inches (23–30 cm)

FOOD
Insects, small reptiles,
vegetation

HABITAT
Open, rocky areas; coastal
woodlands; savanna;
urban areas

RANGE
Sub-Saharan Africa

If this lizard were named after the female of the species, it wouldn't be called the rainbow agama. The female is a dull brown with patches of color on her skin. It's the male who is a rainbow, with a blue or purple body and a head that's red or orange, with the color sometimes spilling down into his shoulders, forelegs, and sides. His tail is wrapped in bands of color, too.

Not all males are this colorful, though. The cloak of many colors is worn by the dominant male, who also gets to perch in the highest, best place among the rocks in the territory he shares with a few females and younger males. These other lizards must settle for second best. But even a multicolored male sometimes loses his hues. At night, or when it's cool, he tones down to a grayer shade.

If a dominant male is challenged, a fight erupts. The lizards bite and lash each other with their tails. An agama's tail makes up more than half its length, so it's a formidable weapon—unless it gets broken during battle. Many older male agamas have shortened tails as a result of a lifetime of fights. The victorious male will gleam with bright colors while the loser skulks away in a drab gray-brown uniform.

Rainbow agamas are active predators. They scurry after insects and even jump into the air to snare flying insects.

A female rainbow agama lays up to eight eggs in a hole she digs in damp soil. Temperature controls whether hatchlings are male or female: At or above 84°F (29°C), they will be male.

AGAMA AGAMA

6,50s

République de Guinée

The rainbow agama is also known as the "house agama" because it's often found basking on walls and buildings in towns. In 1997, the familiar lizard was put on a stamp produced by the Republic of Guinea in Africa.

Frilled lizards vary in color from gray to brown across their range. Their frills have orange and black markings in some areas. When the frills are folded, they look like capes.

In 2013, Australia put a frilled lizard on the first coin in a set of collectible silver coins featuring Australian reptiles.

FRILLED NECK LIZARD

FRILLED LIZARD

Most of the time, the frilled lizard putters along, minding its own business as it hunts for insects and other small prey. It looks like nothing more than a large lizard with a droopy shawl on its neck. But let a predator approach, and watch out! Suddenly the lizard stands up on its hind legs, opens its mouth wide, and hisses while big flaps spring open on either side of its head.

This threat display is enough to stop many predators in their tracks, such as the dingo, a wild dog of Australia. While the startled predator pauses, the lizard quickly runs away, still on its hind legs. Those legs whirl so quickly that they've earned the lizard the nickname "bicycle lizard"! The lizard sprints until it reaches a tree where it can climb to safety.

Up a tree is where frilled lizards prefer to be, anyway. They climb down only when they spot insect prey. Then they march across the ground on their hind legs as they hunt. Females lay their eggs in underground nests. During the dry season, the lizards curl up in holes high in the trees to estivate (sleep through a hot, dry season) until wetter weather returns.

Both male and female lizards have frills, though males are bigger overall. Males spread their frills at other males during mating season in tussles over territory. The frills may also help the lizards soak up sunshine when they're cold and lose heat when they're too hot.

FAMILY
Agamidae

FACTS

OTHER COMMON NAMES
Australian frilled lizard, frilled dragon, frillneck

SCIENTIFIC NAME
Chlamydosaurus kingii

SIZE
24–35 inches (60–90 cm)

FOOD
Insects, sometimes small lizards and mammals

HABITAT
Dry forests and woodlands

RANGE
Northern Australia, southern New Guinea

FLYING DRAGON

For a lizard, scuttling down a tree trunk and across the ground to get to another tree can be a dangerous journey. It risks being caught by a ground-dwelling predator. Climbing also uses up energy. But as its name suggests, the flying dragon avoids both these problems by soaring from tree to tree.

The flying dragon doesn't actually have wings, nor does it flap. It's a glider. Sticking out from its sides are pairs of extra-long ribs that are covered with a thin membrane. They're a bit like the ribs of an umbrella with fabric stretched in between. The ribby membrane is called a patagium. At rest, both patagia are folded up. When it's time to glide, the dragon spreads them open, then jumps into the air from a high perch in a tree. As it glides downhill, it steers with its long tail, until finally it lands on a branch or trunk. A dragon can glide about 30 feet (9 m)—and sometimes more! Glides of up to 56 feet (17 m) have been observed.

The common flying dragon's wings are orange with dark markings. There are more than 40 species of dragon, who flash other wing colors such as yellow and blue. For a lizard that zips around like this, it's interesting to learn that it typically sits and waits for ants to walk by, slurping them up without budging.

A flying dragon's "wings" are supported by long ribs. The flaps are not attached to its limbs, unlike the loose skin of a Kuhl's flying gecko (pages 64–65), which is attached to the front and back legs and stretches between them.

A male flying dragon has a large flap, or dewlap, on his neck that he can extend like a flag. He opens and shuts this "flag" while courting female dragons. He can also use it to threaten other males that enter his territory.

A female sailfin lays eggs along the bank of a river or stream, carefully burying them where the water won't reach if there is a flood. The eggs would not survive underwater.

Got frills? Dimetrodons did. These prehistoric animals lived before dinosaurs. It was once widely thought that the dimetrodon's sail was used to regulate its body temperature, but the sail's supersizing suggests that it was for display, much like a peacock's tail.

PHILIPPINE SAILFIN LIZARD

The sailfin lizard is named after the large fin at the base of the male's tail. The female's fin is much smaller. Both male and female have fringed toes, like the basilisk lizard (pages 84–85). Adult sailfins don't run, but the little, lightweight sailfin hatchlings are excellent sprinters. The youngsters use their ability to run on water to escape birds, snakes, and other predators.

Most of the time, a sailfin hangs out in trees that drape over streams and rivers. If a predator creeps along its branch, the sailfin simply drops into the water and swims to the bottom, where it can hide for up to 15 minutes. Like other aquatic lizards, a sailfin swims by moving its tail from side to side. The tail's flattened shape makes it a perfect oar.

The sailfin's sail isn't used for sailing, so what's it for? One hypothesis is that it helps the lizard regulate its body temperature. By exposing the wide, thin sail to sunlight, the lizard can soak up more heat. Likewise, a cool breeze brushing against the sail can whisk away heat if the lizard is too warm. But why, then, are the male's sails so much bigger? The sail likely plays a role in threat displays to other males and courtship displays to females.

FAMILY
Agamidae

FACTS

OTHER COMMON NAMES
Crested lizard, sail-fin lizard, water dragon, soa-soa water lizard

SCIENTIFIC NAME
Hydrosaurus pustulatus

SIZE
2.5–3 feet (0.8–1 m)

FOOD
Leaves, flowers, fruit, insects, fish, frogs

HABITAT
Streamside and riverside forests

RANGE
Philippines

93

THORNY DEVIL

FACTS

OTHER COMMON NAMES
Thorny dragon, thorny lizard, mountain devil, moloch

SCIENTIFIC NAME
Moloch horridus

SIZE
6–7 inches (15–18 cm)

FOOD
Ants

HABITAT
Deserts

RANGE
Western and central Australia

No reptile is as spiky as the thorny devil! Sharp spines cover its body from snout to tail. If the lizard meets a predator, it tucks its head between its front legs, which makes the spiky hump on its neck stick out. Few animals care to swallow such a prickly meal! Big lizards and birds, however, are known to eat these lizards.

The spikes aren't just for protection. They also help the thorny devil obtain water in its dry desert habitat. The spikes and skin are lined with tiny grooves. These grooves channel water from anywhere on the body to the corners of the lizard's mouth. Rain, dew, and even water absorbed from moist sand flows along these grooves. This plumbing system is so efficient, a thorny devil's entire skin will grow damp shortly after just the tip of its tail is dipped into water.

Thorny devils are certainly thorny, but they're not devils. They're very calm, slow-moving little lizards. They live on a diet of ants. A feast for a thorny devil means sitting beside an ant trail, picking up the scurrying insects one at a time with a sticky tongue. A thorny devil can eat 25 to 45 ants per minute. At this rate, it can consume up to 2,500 ants in one meal.

Australia's thorny devil and North America's horned lizard have both evolved similar bodies and behaviors to survive in their hot, dry habitats. They are an example of convergent evolution—a process in which two animals living in similar habitats independently evolve similar traits.

Thorny devils change color depending on activity level and temperature. A warm, busy lizard is yellow, tan, and red. A cold or scared one turns dark brown or olive green.

A chameleon's foot has two fused toes on one side and three fused toes on the other. These mittenlike feet are adapted to help the chameleon clamp onto branches and walk along them.

This chameleon's big horns clearly mark him as a male. A female Jackson's may have a nose horn with or without small horns on her head—or no horns at all. Males may be all green or have some blue on their heads and some yellow on their sides.

JACKSON'S CHAMELEON

A male Jackson's chameleon looks like a cross between a rhinoceros and a bull. Two big horns stick out of his head above his eyes. A third pokes out of his nose. When two males confront each other on a branch, they use their horns to shove and jab at each other, head to head. Each one tries to push his opponent off the branch.

A female Jackson's doesn't have big horns, but like the male she has a shield, called a casque, on her head. She is a member of a special club: Most chameleons lay eggs, but the Jackson's is among the few species that give live birth. She carries the developing eggs inside her body for up to six months. The eggs hatch at the time of laying, producing a litter of as many as 40 babies.

Jackson's chameleons are native to East Africa, but Hawaii, U.S.A., is now home to them, too. In 1972, a few dozen chameleons escaped from the backyard of a pet store in that state. They thrived in the Hawaiian forest, which was very similar to their East African habitat. Hawaii does not have any native land-based reptile species, so escapees and their descendants are considered pests. Laws are in place to prevent the chameleons from spreading across the state. It's illegal, for example, to transport reptiles from island to island.

FAMILY
Chamaeleonidae

FACTS

OTHER COMMON NAMES
Three-horned chameleon

SCIENTIFIC NAME
Trioceros jacksonii

SIZE
8–12 inches (20–30 cm)

FOOD
Insects, spiders, snails

HABITAT
Mountain forests

RANGE
East Africa, Hawaii

Many chameleons sport "horns," but the Jackson's is one of the few that has a bony core inside its horns. Most chameleon horns are scaly, flexible structures that grow from the skin, like the one on the snout of the long-nosed chameleon.

VEILED CHAMELEON

A veiled chameleon's pointy casque makes it look as if it's wearing a helmet. Chameleon casques range from small, barely visible bumps to large, showy headgear. The male veiled chameleon has the largest casque of any chameleon species.

The casque also turns spectacular colors, as does the body, when a male chameleon threatens another male trespassing on his territory. If flashing his colors, coiling his tail, and pinching with his feet doesn't drive off the intruder, the male may resort to butting heads and biting.

The veiled chameleon lives in trees and bushes, where it feeds on insects and drinks from water droplets on leaves. During dry seasons it may eat the leaves, too, because they contain water in their cells. With its flat body shape and green color, the chameleon looks like a leaf itself, especially when it rocks gently on a branch as if blowing in the breeze.

Veiled chameleons are sometimes kept as pets, but they are not easy to care for, and they cause problems when they escape. Veiled chameleons that have escaped are now found in places such as Florida and Hawaii, U.S.A., where they prey on native species of insects as well as on small birds.

A female veiled chameleon may turn lime green with blue and orange spots to show a male chameleon that he's welcome to approach.

A "gravid" female—one that's already mated and is carrying eggs—turns dark green with blue and yellow spots to tell a male to get lost.

Veiled chameleon hatchlings are pale green. In the wild, only some hatchlings survive to adulthood because chameleons are preyed upon by animals such as birds and snakes.

Panther chameleons are loners! They don't hang out with others of their kind except during breeding season. A male won't let another male trespass in his tree—he turns bright warning colors and chases the intruder, even fighting him if necessary.

In 2012, scientists announced the discovery of four new chameleon species on Madagascar. The little animals are leaf chameleons, which spend the day in leaf litter on the forest floor. At night they creep up into shrubs. *Brookesia micra,* which was among their finds, is so small that a hatchling can perch on the tip of a match!

PANTHER CHAMELEON

Dazzling and different! Panther chameleons, which live on the island of Madagascar, are among the most colorful chameleons in the world. A normally bright green chameleon can put on a fireworks display of yellow, red, orange, and other colors. This species' colors also vary from place to place. In one area, for example, lizards are bright blue; in another they are a radiant red.

Females, however, are usually brown with shades of pink or orange all over. A female that is carrying eggs, however, may turn dark brown or black with pink or orange bars to warn males to keep their distance.

Madagascar is a chameleon-lover's paradise. It's home to almost half the world's known species of chameleon, including about 60 that are found nowhere else. This chameleon collection includes the world's smallest species, *Brookesia micra,* which is only about an inch (2.5 cm) long, as well as one of the longest, Oustalet's chameleon, which can measure up to 27 inches (68 cm) long.

Many old superstitions surround chameleons in Madagascar. Some people think touching one or stepping over one is bad luck. For the island's chameleons, the real bad luck is being collected illegally for the pet trade and losing habitat when forests are cut down.

FAMILY
Chamaeleonidae

FACTS

OTHER COMMON NAMES
None

SCIENTIFIC NAME
Furcifer pardalis

SIZE
16–22 inches
(40–56 cm)

FOOD
Insects

HABITAT
Lowland forests

RANGE
Madagascar

SHINGLEBACK SKINK

FAMILY
Scincidae

OTHER COMMON NAMES
Bobtail, boggi, stump-tailed skink, pinecone lizard, sleepy lizard, two-headed skink

SCIENTIFIC NAME
Tiliqua rugosa

SIZE
12–16 inches (30–41 cm)

FOOD
Insects, snails, leaves

HABITAT
Dry grasslands, woodlands

RANGE
Australia

A two-headed lizard? No, just a shingleback skink— a lizard that fools its predators with its double-ended disguise! A shingleback's short, plump tail looks so much like its head that a predator may be tricked into attacking the wrong end. This mistake gives the skink an extra few seconds to defend itself or find a hiding place. Unlike many lizards, however, it can't shed its tail in a last-ditch effort to escape.

The shingleback is one of several species of blue-tongued skinks in Australia. These skinks stick out their blue tongue at predators in order to threaten them. It's not that the predators are shocked by the skink's rudeness—they're startled by the tongue's sudden appearance and the way its dark color contrasts with the pink mouth lining. The skink's hissing and puffed-up body add to the surprise. If the predator persists, the skink backs up its threat by biting.

Shinglebacks exhibit a rare form of behavior in the reptile world: long-lasting "pair bonds." A male and female shingleback hang out together before, during, and (for a short time) after the spring breeding season. They also keep pairing up, year after year, sometimes for their entire lives. Researchers have noted pairs that remained couples for about 20 years!

A female shingleback typically gives live birth to one or two very big youngsters, though sometimes she may have three or even four.

A defensive shingleback often curls its body so that its head and look-alike tail are both shown to an animal that approaches it.

103

A baby red-eyed crocodile skink is dark with a pale or yellow head and markings. It develops the "goggles" around its eyes as it grows.

Coconut piles are home to a variety of animals in addition to crocodile skinks and insects. Rats and small mammals called bandicoots live in them, too, as do various snakes.

RED-EYED CROCODILE SKINK

A tiny crocodile wearing spectacles that makes sounds a bit like a crying baby? It's for real! The red-eyed crocodile skink is a little lizard that lives in leaf litter on the rain forest floor. It also lives in piles of coconut husks on coconut farms. The husks are removed from the hard-shelled coconuts, then tossed into waste piles. They make cool, moist homes for these skinks.

The crocodile skink's famous cry is a high-pitched, creaking, screeching sound. It yelps when it's scared or angry. The female will also yelp to protect her egg. She lays just one long, oval, leathery egg at a time. After laying the egg, the female sticks close to it when she's not feeding. She will screech and lunge with her mouth wide open to protect the egg. She will also protect the tiny hatchling after it emerges.

Crocodile skinks are unusual in many other ways, too. The ridge of pointy scales on their backs is not something you see on most skinks. Neither is the helmet, or casque, on its head. Males also have little bumps called pores on their hind feet. The pores are thought to leave scents for marking territory.

FAMILY
Scincidae

FACTS

OTHER COMMON NAMES
Orange-eyed crocodile skink, helmeted skink, red-eyed bush crocodile, casque-headed skink

SCIENTIFIC NAME
Tribolonotus gracilis

SIZE
8–10 inches (20–25 cm)

FOOD
Insects

HABITAT
Tropical forests

RANGE
New Guinea, Indonesia, Solomon Islands

BLUE-TAILED SKINK

FACTS

OTHER COMMON NAMES
Blue-tailed snake-eyed skink, Christmas Island blue-tailed skink

SCIENTIFIC NAME
Cryptoblepharus egeriae

SIZE
1.6–3 inches (4–8 cm)

FOOD
Insects, worms

HABITAT
Rain forest, woodland

RANGE
Christmas Island

The blue-tailed skink's bright blue tail is eye-catching—even more so when it pops off the skink! This trick, which is widespread among reptiles, leaves a predator with a twitching tail while the skink makes a getaway.

Unfortunately for the blue-tailed skink, its predators have increased over the past few decades. In the past, it only needed to avoid a few predators native to its remote Australian island (for example, two species of rats, now extinct). People who came to the island, however, brought non-native species that quickly invaded the skinks' home. These predators included pets such as cats as well as stowaways on ships and planes such as yellow crazy ants, Asian wolf snakes, giant centipedes, and black rats.

The skink, once common across the island, is now rare, and some experts think it may be extinct in the wild. There are captive collections of skinks, which could one day be used to supply new skinks to Christmas Island if the invasive species can be controlled and the habitat protected.

The forest skink once lived on Christmas Island, too. In the 1990s, a person could see nearly a hundred of them hanging out on a log. By 2012, there was just one forest skink left, a female named Gump living in captivity.

America is home to many species of blue-tailed skinks. Despite the resemblance, these skinks are not closely related to the Christmas Island skink.

A female armadillo girdled lizard typically gives live birth to one baby at a time. It's a big baby, too—nearly half as long as she is!

The armadillo girdled lizard is named after the armadillo, a mammal that also rolls up in a ball to protect itself.

ARMADILLO GIRDLED LIZARD

Armadillo girdled lizards live among rocks in areas where there are termite mounds.

Termites are one of this lizard's main foods. To catch termites, a girdled lizard trundles away from the safety of the nooks and crannies among the rocks. Running this errand is a dangerous mission for a little lizard, even one as heavily armored with spiky scales as this one is! Hungry birds can easily snap up the slow-moving reptile. To ward off attacks, the girdled lizard has a unique defense. It quickly rolls into a ball, so that its tender belly is protected by its curled, prickly body. It even bites its tail to keep itself tightly rolled up. In this position, the lizard not only protects its body but also becomes an awkward thing to swallow. It can remain curled up like this for about an hour, during which time a predator is likely to wander off and find something easier to eat.

Armadillo girdled lizards do something else that's unique: They live in large groups. As many as 30 lizards may share the same rocky area, sleeping in its crevices at night and basking on boulders by day. These lizards aren't all part of the same family. They are just sharing the same food and shelter, though they may benefit by living in groups because there are more eyes watching out for danger.

FAMILY
Cordylidae

FACTS

OTHER COMMON NAMES
Armadillo lizard, golden armadillo lizard, blinkogie, armadillo spiny-tailed lizard

SCIENTIFIC NAME
Ouroborus cataphractus

SIZE
6–8 inches (16–21 cm)

FOOD
Insects

HABITAT
Rocky deserts, dry scrublands

RANGE
Western South Africa

SLOW WORM

FAMILY
Anguidae

FACTS

OTHER COMMON NAMES
Blind worm, dead adder

SCIENTIFIC NAME
Anguis fragilis

SIZE
12–16 inches (30-40 cm)

FOOD
Snails, slugs, worms

HABITAT
Woods, gardens, grasslands

RANGE
Europe, Asia, northern Africa

Like the snake-lizard (pages 66–67), the slow worm is a reptile without legs that resembles a snake. But it's neither a worm nor a snake. It's a lizard superbly adapted for a life of burrowing.

Its body is covered with smooth scales that don't overlap. This adaptation helps a slow worm slip through loose soil as well as leaf litter and grass. This is a lizard you're not likely to see basking on a rock—it is very secretive and prefers to remain hidden under rocks, dead leaves, paving stones, and logs or inside a burrow or compost heap.

Slow worms usually move slowly, and their prey is just as slow! Slow worms specialize in eating slugs and snails. They are welcome predators in a garden, where they gobble up pests that would otherwise eat vegetables and flowers. Gardeners who let their cats outside, however, don't benefit from the slow worms' help, because cats prey on these lizards.

A male slow worm is light or dark brown, gray, rusty red, or copper in color and has a belly with dark blotches. Some males have blue spots on their sides. The female typically has a stripe along her back, dark spots on her sides, and a dark belly.

Life in the slow lane suits slow worms. They're among the longest-living lizards, known to survive for about 30 years in the wild. One slow worm in a zoo lived for 54 years!

The slow worm's scientific name, *Anguis fragilis,* means "brittle snake." It refers to the lizard's tail, which snaps off easily if it's attacked by a predator.

A female slow worm gives birth to tiny youngsters with black undersides in late summer.

The beaded lizard of Mexico is venomous, too. It is black with yellow markings and can grow to be 3 feet (1 m) long.

A female Gila monster lays eggs in a burrow in the fall. They hatch the following spring. This species is the only North American lizard known to lay eggs that wait all winter to hatch the next year.

GILA MONSTER

The Gila monster is one of a few known species of venomous lizard. Its venom glands lie in its lower jaw. The venom flows out through grooves in the teeth. Unlike most venomous snakes, which bite quickly and let go, a Gila monster must hang on and chew to make its venom ooze into its victim's bloodstream.

A Gila monster's venom is used as a defense against predators, not for hunting. It doesn't need venom to subdue its meals, which consist mostly of reptile and bird eggs, baby rodents, baby birds, and insects, with the occasional frog or lizard and bites of already-dead animals' bodies. It finds food by sniffing it out with its sharp sense of smell, which is aided by the flicking of its sensitive tongue.

The Gila monster is the biggest lizard native to the United States. It can be 22 inches (56 cm) long and weigh about 5 pounds (2.3 kg). Some of this weight is due to its plump tail, which stores food as fat. A well-fed monster looks like a plump sausage! When food is scarce, its body uses up the stored fat and the tail may shrink to four-fifths its usual size.

Though a monster looks clumsy, it can climb a cactus to reach a bird's nest and gobble up the eggs. It has a monstrous appetite and can eat up to a third of its weight in one meal. But it doesn't need to eat often. It can survive on less than a dozen big meals in one year.

FAMILY
Helodermatidae

FACTS

OTHER COMMON NAMES
None

SCIENTIFIC NAME
Heloderma suspectum

SIZE
12–22 inches (30–56 cm)

FOOD
Insects, worms, lizards, rodent young, baby birds, eggs

HABITAT
Deserts, dry grasslands

RANGE
Southwestern United States and northwestern Mexico

KOMODO DRAGON

Want to check out the world's heaviest, biggest lizard? Look no further than the Komodo dragon! This giant lizard can be up to 10 feet (3 m) long and weigh 150 pounds (68 kg) or more. It's so big, it preys on animals such as water buffalo, deer, horses, and pigs.

A Komodo dragon roams its island home in search of prey or ambushes animals that walk past it when it's hiding. It leaps out and attacks the animal's legs or seizes its neck, bites with sharp teeth, and slashes with sharp claws. If its victim somehow escapes, the dragon doesn't care. Its jaw contains venom glands, which ooze venom into the wounds made by its teeth. The venom prevents blood from clotting, so any animal that stumbles away eventually bleeds to death.

Then the dragon tracks it down, flicking its forked tongue to sample the air and pick up the scent of the dead animal. A dragon can smell carrion (rotting meat) even if it is 2.5 miles (4 km) away. Then it will feast. A dragon can devour about 80 percent of its body weight in just one meal, gulping down meat so fast that it can swallow 5.5 pounds (2.5 kg) every minute!

For many decades, it was thought that the dragon's prey died because their wounds were infected with bacteria from the dragon's mouth. The discovery of the venom glands and further studies of Komodo dragon saliva showed that this isn't the case.

A female dragon lays eggs in a hole she digs in a hillside or the ground. She may also lay them in the nests of scrub fowl, which build big heaps of leaves, sticks, and dirt for their eggs.

Sometimes a group of dragons shows up to devour a large carcass, much as vultures do. The dragons smell carrion from afar and travel from different places to feed on it.

The perentie and other monitor lizards can stand on their hind legs and lean on their tails to check out their surroundings, as this yellow-spotted monitor is doing.

A female perentie lays her eggs in a burrow or a termite nest. Termites work hard to keep their nests warm and humid, which makes them a cozy place for eggs, too!

PERENTIE

Australia's biggest lizard is the perentie, a cousin of the Komodo dragon (pages 114–115).

They're both in the "varanid lizard" family. But a varanid bigger than either lizard once roamed Australia. Scientists have found fossils of a gigantic varanid 15 feet (4.6 m) long! Supersize Komodo dragons bigger than modern ones lived in Australia, too. These animals appear to have gone extinct about 40,000 years ago.

The perentie was traditionally a favorite food of Australia's original inhabitants, known as the Aboriginal people. Its name comes from the word *pirrinthi*, an Aboriginal name for the lizard. Perenties appear in ancient Aboriginal art and stories, and modern Aboriginal artists continue to use these big lizards as subjects in their works.

Perenties are wary and quick to hide in burrows when they see people. Their big claws help them dig quickly into the desert soil. Unlike their Komodo dragon cousins, adult perenties can also climb trees.

What a perentie eats depends on its size. Hatchlings go after insects; the biggest full-grown perenties can tackle small kangaroos! Smaller prey is often killed by rapidly shaking it to death, just as a dog might shake a squirrel or rabbit. Like its cousin, the perentie was once thought to kill prey with a bacteria-infected bite, but it is now thought to produce venom.

FAMILY
Varanidae

FACTS

OTHER COMMON NAMES
Giant monitor lizard, goanna

SCIENTIFIC NAME
Varanus giganteus

SIZE
5–6.5 feet (1.5–2 m)

FOOD
Eggs, insects, fish, reptiles, birds, rabbits, small kangaroos, carrion

HABITAT
Dry lands, deserts

RANGE
Australia

SCHELTO-PUSIK

FAMILY
Anguidae

FACTS

OTHER COMMON NAMES
European legless lizard,
European glass lizard

SCIENTIFIC NAME
Pseudopus apodus

SIZE
2–4 feet (0.6–1.2 m)

FOOD
Insects, lizards, rodents,
snails, slugs, spiders,
centipedes

HABITAT
Woods, grasslands, and
rocky, dry hillsides

RANGE
Southern Europe,
Central Asia

The scheltopusik is another of those snakelike lizards that keep people guessing. Ear openings and eyes that blink are among the clues that this reptile isn't a snake. It also has tiny stumps at its hind end, all that are left of the legs its ancestors had. It is Europe's largest species of legless lizard.

Like many lizards, the scheltopusik can shed its tail if attacked, but because of its large size it tends to fight back by hissing and biting instead. Most of its size, however, is made up of tail. The tail is about two-thirds of the lizard's entire length, and it doesn't just pop off to distract a predator: The long, cast-off tail also breaks into smaller, wriggling pieces. Suddenly, the predator is confronted with several "lizards" where before it saw just one! The scheltopusik can escape while the confused predator tries to figure out which piece is the body.

This weird ability explains the scheltopusik's common name of "glass lizard" because people used to think the whole animal could shatter like glass. In some places, people even believed that the broken bits would later rejoin the body to form a whole lizard again! Of course, this doesn't happen, though the lizard does regrow its tail. The name "scheltopusik," however, simply means "yellow-bellied" in Russian.

A scheltopusik isn't as flexible as a snake. A snake's skin stretches more than a lizard's does so it can expand easily when it swallows prey. A scheltopusik's skin is stiffer. However, it has stretchy grooves down its side that work like an elastic waistband for its body, allowing it to expand just enough to make room for a big meal.

A female scheltopusik lays her eggs under a stone, a log, or other shelter. She guards the eggs until they hatch, and she will lunge and snap at any threats.

VIỆT NAM
DÂN CHỦ CỘNG HOÀ

BƯU CHÍNH

12 ×

RỒNG ĐẤT   PHYSIGNATHUS COCINCINUS

The Chinese water dragon actually lives in many parts of Asia, including Vietnam. In 1975, North Vietnam honored the lizard by putting it on a stamp.

The Chinese water dragon is the only species in its genus, *Physignathus.*

CHINESE WATER DRAGON

About two-thirds of a Chinese water dragon's length is made up of its tail. Like many aquatic reptiles, the water dragon uses its tail to swim. It also uses its tail as a whip to lash out at predators.

Like the plumed basilisk (pages 84–85), a water dragon can run on just its two powerful hind legs, but it can't run on water. Instead, it drops from its tree branch when frightened, dives deep in the water, and hides there. It can hold its breath and remain underwater for up to 25 minutes. As its name implies, the water dragon feels right at home in the water. It swims quickly enough to catch fish.

On top of its head, a water dragon has a tiny, round, shiny spot. This spot is called the pineal body or "third eye." It is a clear, light-sensitive lid connected to a bundle of nerves that leads to the brain through a small gap in the skull. It allows the lizard to sense slight differences in light levels. This ability helps its body tune in to the rhythm of day and night and also to adjust its body temperature. The pineal body may even help it react quickly to the shadow of a hungry bird! Many other lizards have a pineal body, too.

FAMILY
Agamidae

FACTS

OTHER COMMON NAMES
Asian water dragon, Thai water dragon, green water dragon

SCIENTIFIC NAME
Physignathus cocincinus

SIZE
2–3 feet (0.6–1 m)

FOOD
Leaves, eggs, insects, fish, birds, small mammals

HABITAT
Near rain forest rivers, lakes, ponds, and swamps

RANGE
Thailand, Vietnam, Laos, Cambodia, Myanmar, China

ALL ABOUT SNAKES

Snakes are in the order Squamata along with lizards and amphisbaenians.

There are about 3,500 species, and, as with other squamates, new ones are being discovered all the time. In 2010, for example, researchers discovered a brightly colored vine snake new to science. They found the snake, which they named *Chironius challenger,* in an Amazonian mountainside rain forest.

To date, scientists haven't yet discovered exactly which reptile is the ancestor of all snakes. Researchers continue to study fossils for clues. It was once widely thought that snakes descended from an eel-like lizard that swam in the ocean. Today, studies seem to suggest that snakes may have evolved from lizards that burrowed on land.

No snake has legs, though some species have small spurs on their hind ends— all that remain of their distant ancestors' limbs. But the absence of legs isn't the only thing that distinguishes a snake from a lizard—after all, there are legless lizards! A snake's skull, for example, is constructed so that the snake can dislocate its lower jaw in order to stretch its jaws around its prey. The front of the lower jaw is also not connected by bone. It is linked in front by a stretchy band of tissue instead. This allows a snake to swallow food whole, without chewing.

Also, a snake's skeleton is basically just a skull connected to a long spine and lots of ribs. Some species have up to 400 pairs of ribs! The body is packed with muscles that connect to the ribs so the snake can slither, swim, and climb. It lacks the shoulder and pelvic (hip) bones of lizards, though a few species have leftover fragments of pelvic bones. Snakes also lack movable eyelids and external ear openings. They all have forked tongues.

Blue Malaysian coral snake
(Calliophis bivirgata)
The blue Malaysian coral snake waves its red tail and even flips upside down to display its red underside to warn off predators.

Copperhead
(Agkistrodon contortrix)
The copperhead of North America is a venomous snake named for its orange-brown head.

Elephant-trunk snake
(Acrochordus javanicus)
The elephant-trunk snake lives in rivers and streams. It has baggy, rough skin. It's also called the Javan wart snake or file snake.

Horned viper
(Cerastes cerastes)
The horned viper hides in the sand of the Sahara desert by day. It suddenly leaps out of hiding to catch prey.

Common death adder
(Acanthophis antarcticus)
This venomous snake lives in Australia and Papua New Guinea. An ambush predator, the snake waits for prey while hiding itself in sand, soil, or leaves.

Coachwhip
(Masticophis flagellum)
The coachwhip of North America ranges from tan to black in color. It can be up to 5 feet (1.5 m) long.

Banded krait
(Bungarus fasciatus)
The venomous banded krait of Southeast Asia hides by day. At night, it hunts rats, lizards, and other snakes.

Mozambique spitting cobra
(Naja mossambica)
This poisonous snake can spit venom up to 8 feet (2.4 m) away.

AFRICAN ROCK PYTHON

Africa's largest snake is the rock python, which can grow so large it can tackle a crocodile. It often lurks in or near streams, marshes, lakes, and rivers, waiting to ambush animals that come down to the water to drink. Prey is seized and held with the teeth as the python coils its powerful body around it.

Many people think a python kills its prey by crushing it, but this isn't true. A python actually suffocates its prey. It does so by tightening its squeeze every time the victim exhales. With every breath out, the prey is held more firmly in the python's coils. Eventually, it's held so tightly that it can't expand its rib cage to breathe in any more. A snake that kills in this way is called a constrictor—it constricts the movement and breathing of its prey.

A big meal satisfies a python for many days. It stops hunting and spends its time digesting its meal in a sheltered spot. If necessary, it can live for months without food.

The rock python avoids the hottest part of the day by hunting mainly during the morning and evening. During the dry season, this python estivates inside a log, a hollow tree, or a burrow abandoned by another animal.

An African rock python can swallow meals much bigger than its head. Here, one takes down a whole Thomson's gazelle in a dramatic display of the flexibility of a python's jaw structure.

A female rock python may lay up to 100 eggs. She coils around them and guards them fiercely until they hatch about three months later.

In 1999, a biologist studying sun bears on the island of Borneo reported that a reticulated python had eaten a bear. This observation was a scientific first! The bear, however, was small and weak from lack of food, so "bear fare" may be rare for pythons.

"Pit organs" on a reticulated python's face detect heat and allow the snake to see a heat, or "infrared," image of its prey. This ability lets a snake sense prey in dim or dark places, or even on a pitch-black night.

RETICULATED PYTHON

The world's longest snake, the reticulated python, slithers through rain forests and grasslands of Southeast Asia. The largest reticulated python ever officially recorded—a snake found in Indonesia in 1912—measured 32 feet, 10 inches (10 m) in length. It beats out the green anaconda (pages 134–135) of South America for length, but the anaconda gets the nod as the biggest snake because it's heavier.

The "reticulated" part of the python's name means "netlike" and describes the linked pattern on its skin, which helps it virtually disappear among fallen leaves. Reticulated pythons can hide in plain sight and ambush passing prey, though they also stalk prey. In water, they seize animals coming to drink. Like African rock pythons, they kill by constriction.

Female reticulated pythons coil around their eggs to guard them until they hatch. These huge snakes are about 2 feet (0.6 m) long as hatchlings—a length that would be full adult size for many snake species. The hatchlings eat rodents, lizards, birds, and other small animals, graduating to larger prey as they grow.

Though this python's skin camouflages it, it hasn't hidden it from human eyes. Many pythons are collected illegally each year for sale to the pet trade or for their skins to be made into leather. Mining and logging across their range also poses a threat to the survival of these giant snakes.

FAMILY
Pythonidae

FACTS

OTHER COMMON NAMES
Regal python

SCIENTIFIC NAME
Python reticulatus

SIZE
20–30 feet (6–9 m)

FOOD
Birds, mammals from rodents to deer

HABITAT
Rain forests, woodlands, grasslands near water

RANGE
Southeast Asia

BURMESE PYTHON

FAMILY
Pythonidae

FACTS

OTHER COMMON NAMES
Asian rock python, tiger python

SCIENTIFIC NAME
Python bivittatus

SIZE
16–23 feet (5–7 m)

FOOD
Reptiles, birds, mammals

HABITAT
Rain forests, woodlands, swamps, marshes, grasslands

RANGE
South and Southeast Asia; Florida

The beefy Burmese python is one of the world's longest snakes. This snake is a constrictor that feeds on birds and small mammals. When it's young, it lives mainly in trees. As an adult, however, it can weigh up to 200 pounds (90 kg), so it gives up treetop life and spends its time on the ground.

This snake is threatened in many areas of the countries where it naturally lives. The cutting of forests has depleted its habitat. It has been hunted for its meat and hides and collected for sale overseas.

In an odd twist, however, the python that is endangered in its homeland is becoming a pest elsewhere. Burmese pythons have invaded parts of Florida, U.S.A., including the wetlands called the Everglades. Scientists suspect that the pythons' ancestors were once-captive snakes that found their way into the wild in the 1980s. Did they escape? Were they released by someone who didn't want them anymore? Nobody knows.

The big pythons gobble up the birds and mammals native to Florida, which aren't adapted to living alongside giant constrictors. The pythons even eat alligators. In 2012, studies showed that the number of mammals living in the Everglades had dropped severely. Estimates for the Burmese python population in Florida range from 30,000 to 100,000 snakes.

Burmese pythons can stay underwater for up to 30 minutes without breathing and can swim for long distances. Scientists are concerned that salty ocean water won't stop pythons from spreading in Florida.

Florida wildlife officials and park rangers have made efforts to rid wildlife areas of Burmese pythons. They fear that they are fighting a losing battle because the snakes are very hard to find.

Green tree python hatchlings are yellow with brown speckles. They wiggle their black tails to lure prey.

The green tree python is famous for having a look-alike: the emerald tree boa (pages 136–137) of South American rain forests. They're both lime green constrictors that coil on branches in the same way. This resemblance is another example of convergent evolution (see page 95).

GREEN TREE PYTHON

By day, the green tree python drapes itself on a branch, with its head lying in the middle of its looped-up body. Its bright green color speckled with flecks of white and yellow helps it blend in with leaves. Camouflage is necessary to avoid being found by a hungry hawk, owl, or monitor lizard!

By night, the python is a hunter. Its large eyes gather every scrap of light while pit organs along its lips sense heat, helping the snake target rodents, lizards, and birds. It may even seize prey while dangling from a branch by its strong tail. Though it prefers life in the treetops, this python sometimes hunts on the ground. Females usually lay eggs in tree holes but may slither down to the ground to lay eggs among the exposed tree roots.

The green tree python doesn't start out bright green. Hatchlings of this species are usually bright yellow. They can also be orange, red, or brown. A single batch of eggs may produce all these colors. By the time they're six months to two years old, the young pythons will have changed into their adult green color. Scientists have noticed that yellow hatchlings hunt near the ground in low branches instead of in treetops. Their color helps camouflage them so they are shielded from sharp-eyed birds.

FAMILY
Pythonidae

FACTS

OTHER COMMON NAMES
Green python, Papuan tree python

SCIENTIFIC NAME
Morelia viridis

SIZE
5–6 feet (1.5–1.8 m)

FOOD
Lizards, small mammals, birds

HABITAT
Tropical rain forests

RANGE
New Guinea, northern Australia

BALL PYTHON

FAMILY

Pythonidae

FACTS

OTHER COMMON NAMES
Royal python

SCIENTIFIC NAME
Python regius

SIZE
3–5 feet (1–1.5 m)

FOOD
Small mammals

HABITAT
Savannas, grasslands,
dry forests

RANGE
West and Central Africa

Many snakes coil up when they feel threatened.
They usually raise their heads to hiss and are clearly ready to strike
if attacked. Not the ball python! When this snake coils up, it forms a
tight ball with its head hidden in the middle. It's so strongly coiled up
that it can even be rolled. Any predator bothering this snake has to
figure out what to do with the sudden appearance of a scaly soccer
ball where its prey once sat!

Usually, however, the ball python is safe in a burrow, where it
spends the day. It also estivates in a burrow to avoid the heat of the
dry season. At night, it emerges to hunt. Pit organs help it sense prey
in the dark. Its meals consist mainly of rodents, which makes it an
important ally for African farmers because many rodents feed on
crops. Like other pythons, it kills by constriction.

In some parts of Africa, this species is honored by villagers and
even considered sacred. The pythons are never harmed and may be
welcomed when they slither into a house. A dead python may even be
buried in a small coffin. Pythons in these places are more fortunate
than those in other areas, where they are killed for their meat and
skins or collected for sale as pets.

Some ball pythons have large areas of white on their skin. These rare "piebald" snakes are found in Togo and Ghana.

The ball python is known as the "royal python" in Europe. The snake earned this name because Cleopatra, a queen in ancient Egypt, is popularly thought to have worn a ball python on her wrist as living jewelry.

The biggest anacondas can capture caimans and swallow them whole! After a meal like this, the snake may not need to eat for a month or more. Caimans, in turn, eat young anacondas.

A green anaconda's eyes and nostrils are on the top of its head. It can hide in water with only a sliver of its head showing, like a crocodile.

GREEN ANACONDA

The green anaconda vies with the reticulated python (pages 126–127) for the prize of "largest snake." Lengthwise, both species are giants that can grow nearly as long as a school bus. Experts have split the prize: The reticulated python gets to be "longest snake" because giants of that species are a little longer than anacondas. But the anaconda wins in the "biggest snake" category: Giants of this species can weigh as much as 550 pounds (250 kg)—nearly twice as much as the python, and about half as much as a horse.

Female anacondas are much bigger than males and have even been known to eat them! A female can be twice as long as a typical male. During breeding season, as many as a dozen males may cluster around a female, vying with each other to be her mate. They may tussle this way for as long as a month.

An anaconda is at home in the water. There it ambushes prey, grabbing the animal with its jaws and flinging muscular coils around the prey's body. Prey ranges from fish, turtles, and birds to large animals such as pigs, deer, and giant rodents called capybaras. This powerful snake is even known to have caught jaguars and small crocodylians called caimans. Like pythons, the anaconda kills by constriction.

FAMILY
Boidae

FACTS

OTHER COMMON NAMES
Anaconda, common anaconda, water boa

SCIENTIFIC NAME
Eunectes murinus

SIZE
20–30 feet (6–9 m)

FOOD
Fish, amphibians, reptiles, birds, mammals including deer and capybaras

HABITAT
Rain forest rivers, swamps, marshes, flooded grasslands

RANGE
Northern South America

EMERALD TREE BOA

FACTS

OTHER COMMON NAMES
Green tree boa

SCIENTIFIC NAME
Corallus caninus

SIZE
4–10 feet (1.2–3 m)

FOOD
Lizards, birds,
small mammals

HABITAT
Lowland rain forests

RANGE
South America

Dangling from a tree in the dark of night, an emerald tree boa lies in wait for rodents and other small animals to wander beneath its branch. Its tail and lower body grip the branch firmly. Deep, sensitive pit organs on its face detect the slightest change in temperature. When the boa senses an increase in that temperature, it shoots out its head and neck and seizes its warm prey.

By day, the emerald tree boa drapes itself in coils on a branch with its head resting on top, just like its "double," the green tree python (pages 130–131), which lives half a world away in New Guinea and Australia. Its bright green skin, flecked with white, camouflages it: The green blends in with leaves while the white resembles spots of sunlight.

Unlike the green tree python, an emerald tree boa almost never comes down from its perch. It not only hunts from a branch but can also eat there, hanging on with its tail while coiling around its prey with its front end. Female emerald tree boas even give birth to live young in the treetops, while green tree pythons lay eggs in a tree hole or among tree roots and curl around them to protect them.

Emerald tree boa hatchlings are brick red, orange, or tan. They slowly turn green over the course of three months to a year.

The emerald tree boa's lips are lined with more heat-sensitive pit organs than those of most boas.

137

A female boa constrictor gives birth to as many as 60 babies at a time.

WINS $1,000

SUNDAY APRIL 1 8PM

PLAY NOW

smithchan.com/monstersnake
#mo_stersnake

About 60 million years ago, snakes longer than a city bus slithered across some of the modern common boa's range. This giant, called *Titanoboa cerrejonensis*, was about 45 feet (13.7 m) long and weighed more than 2,000 pounds (907 kg).

BOA CONSTRICTOR

The green anaconda (pages 134–135) shares some of its range with one of the world's best known snakes, the boa constrictor. These boas are so widely distributed, they've evolved into different subspecies across their range. Scientists recognize about ten subspecies, including *Boa constrictor constrictor*, a boa found in South America. The different subspecies' colors and patterns camouflage them in their habitats.

A boa constrictor can swim just as well as an anaconda, but unlike its supersize cousin, it is typically found on land. It also readily climbs trees. Like an emerald tree boa, a boa constrictor may snatch prey while hanging on to a branch. This species has also been observed hanging in the mouth of a cave to grab bats as they fly out in the evening. Like other boa species, boa constrictors kill prey by constriction.

Boa constrictors are popular pets among reptile fans. This popularity comes at a price though: Some subspecies have become endangered because so many snakes have been collected for the pet trade. Laws have been passed to protect these snakes.

FAMILY
Boidae

FACTS

OTHER COMMON NAMES
Common boa

SCIENTIFIC NAME
Boa constrictor

SIZE
6.5–13 feet (2–4 m)

FOOD
Mammals, birds, lizards

HABITAT
Deserts, grasslands, farm fields, dry woodlands, rain forests

RANGE
Central and South America

TEXAS BLIND SNAKE

A Texas blind snake looks more like a big earthworm than a snake. Its body is covered in smooth, pinkish scales. Its eyes are mere dots, not the fierce, staring eyes of other snakes. Its head is rounded like a worm's, its mouth tiny.

There's a reason the blind snake looks wormlike: It lives underground most of the time. Its blunt head and round body slip easily through loose dirt. Its nearly nonexistent eyes, left over from long-ago ancestors that could see, aren't a weakness—the snake doesn't need vision underground.

When the sun goes down, the blind snake goes on the prowl. This small snake bravely enters ant nests, wriggling past the furious insects to get at their young. The blind snake's attack is aided by a fluid produced in its hind end, which it spreads on its body by squirming. The fluid may hide the snake like a smell version of an invisibility cloak, or it might repel ants. Aboveground, the fluid seems to repel coyotes and other snake-eating predators. Oddly, screech owls have been known to bring live blind snakes back to their nests. But they don't feed them to their young. Instead, the snakes live in the nest with the chicks! One hypothesis for this unusual behavior is that the snakes are being used as a kind of house-cleaning crew, keeping the nest tidy by eating mites and other pests.

The Texas blind snake has a spine on the tip of its tail. It uses the spine to brace itself as it squeezes through the tunnels of termite and ant nests.

The world's smallest snake is the Barbados threadsnake, a species of blind snake found on the island of Barbados. It's less than 4 inches (10 cm) long and about as thick as a piece of spaghetti.

Nonvenomous snakes may be clad in warning colors, too. The harmless scarlet king snake, for example, also lives in the southeastern United States, and is often mistaken for a coral snake.

There's an old rhyme people say to help remember which red, yellow, and black snakes in the United States are venomous and which are not: "Red touch yellow, kill a fellow." But this rhyme does not always work because coral snake patterns vary a lot.

EASTERN CORAL SNAKE

Boldly clad in red, yellow, and black stripes, the eastern coral snake's body is a warning from snout to tail that proclaims, "Don't touch! Stay away!" The warning is no bluff—this snake is venomous, and its bite is dangerous. The venom harms the victim's nervous system and eventually paralyzes its muscles. Fortunately, a person who's bitten can be treated with antivenom, a medicine that fights off the effects of venom.

But the coral snake bites only in self-defense. It is shy and secretive, and much more likely to flee and hide than bite. Even if it's cornered, it will try to trick its opponent rather than bite: It curls its tail so that the tail resembles its head.

The eastern coral snake is one of more than 60 species of coral snake found in the Americas. Other species of coral snake live in Asia and Africa. Like its relatives, the eastern coral snake has short fangs. When coral snakes bite, they hang on and chew to work their venom into the wound.

The coral snake spends most of its time in burrows, under logs, or buried in leaf litter, emerging to feed on prey such as frogs, lizards, and small snakes.

FAMILY
Elapidae

FACTS

OTHER COMMON NAMES
Harlequin coral snake

SCIENTIFIC NAME
Micrurus fulvius

SIZE
20–30 inches (51–76 cm)

FOOD
Small snakes, lizards, frogs

HABITAT
Dry woodlands, swamp edges, scrub areas

RANGE
South-central and southeastern United States, northeastern Mexico

YELLOW-BELLIED SEA SNAKE

The tropical regions of the Pacific and Indian Oceans are ribboned with yellow-bellied sea snakes. This species ranges across the open seas, feeding on fish. It never comes up on land unless it gets accidentally washed ashore. Nor does it prowl the seafloor. It usually swims in just the top 30 feet (9 m) of the ocean. Amazingly, it can breathe through its skin as well as its lungs.

The yellow-bellied sea snake hunts fish by sneaking up on them. It also has another trick—one that takes advantage of a habit of little fish: They often hide in the shade of floating sticks and other objects. The unsuspecting fish will investigate a sea snake that's floating motionlessly near the surface. Motionless, that is, until it suddenly whips its head around and gobbles up its visitors! Sea snakes themselves are attracted to floating debris. They gather by the thousands where ocean currents have pushed large amounts of debris into one area.

To date, scientists don't know of any animals that prey on this venomous snake. Captive fish refuse to eat this species, which suggests that perhaps its flesh is bad-tasting or poisonous.

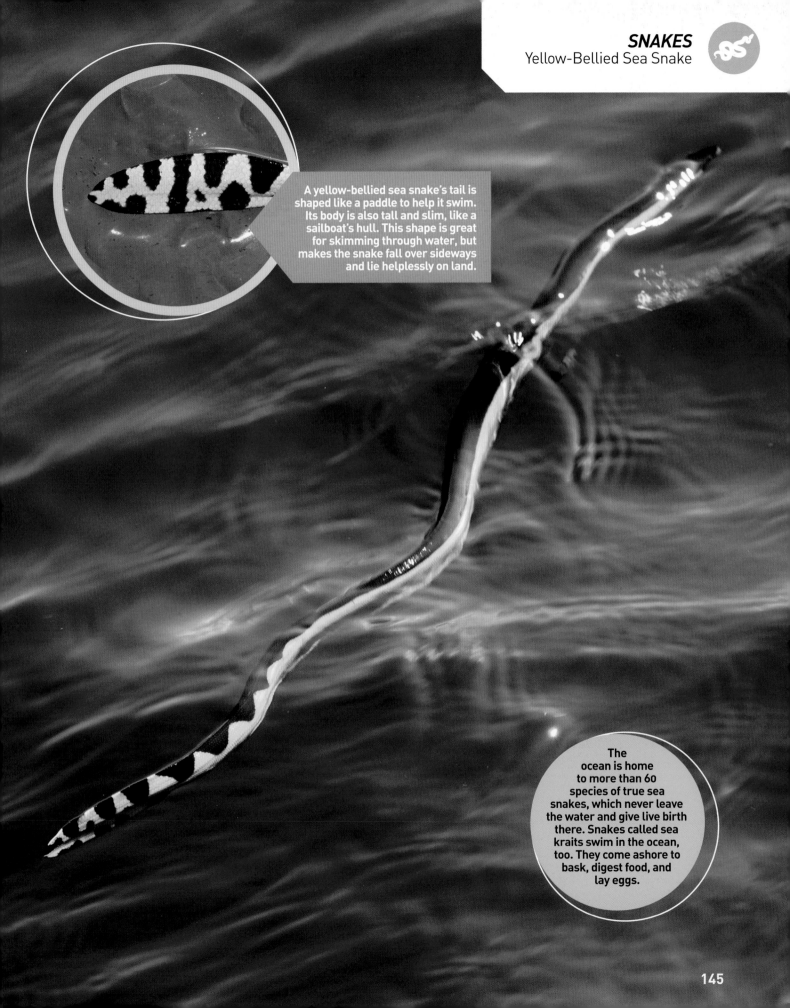

A yellow-bellied sea snake's tail is shaped like a paddle to help it swim. Its body is also tall and slim, like a sailboat's hull. This shape is great for skimming through water, but makes the snake fall over sideways and lie helplessly on land.

The ocean is home to more than 60 species of true sea snakes, which never leave the water and give live birth there. Snakes called sea kraits swim in the ocean, too. They come ashore to bask, digest food, and lay eggs.

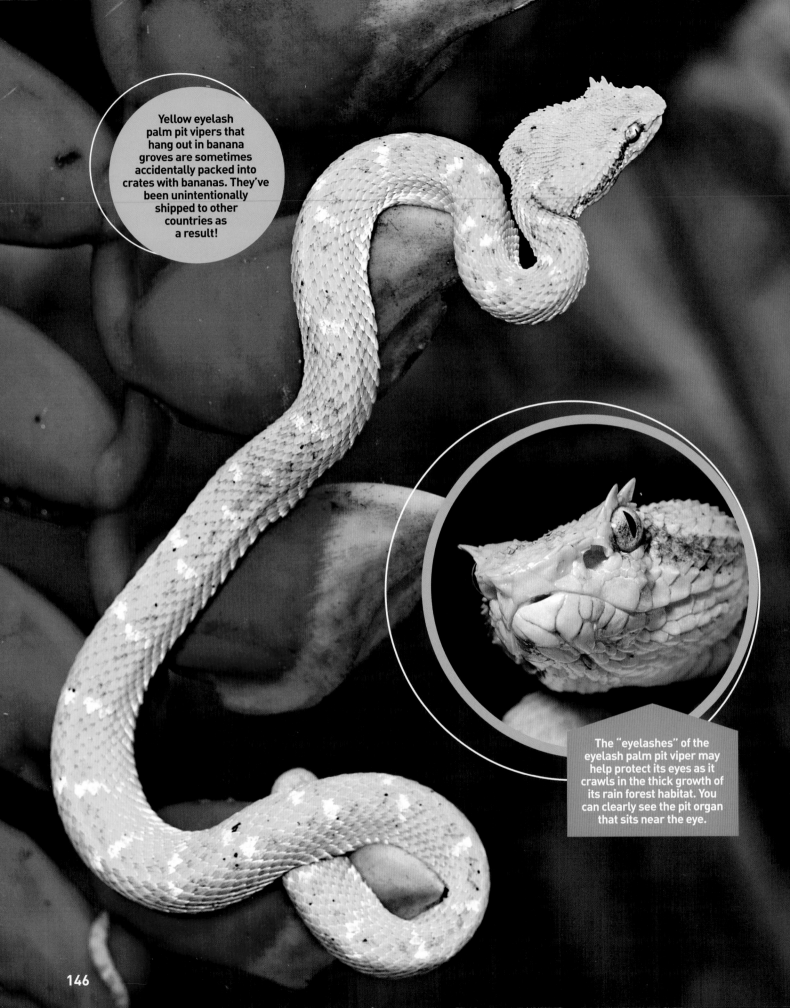

Yellow eyelash palm pit vipers that hang out in banana groves are sometimes accidentally packed into crates with bananas. They've been unintentionally shipped to other countries as a result!

The "eyelashes" of the eyelash palm pit viper may help protect its eyes as it crawls in the thick growth of its rain forest habitat. You can clearly see the pit organ that sits near the eye.

EYELASH PALM PIT VIPER

There's a lot of information packed into the name of the eyelash palm pit viper! The "eyelash" part refers to the spiky scales above its eyes, which look like eyelashes. Folktales in parts of South America claim that the viper winks and bats its eyelashes after it bites. This is an impossible trick, because like all snakes, it lacks movable eyelids.

The "palm" part suggests that it's an arboreal species—a snake that lives in trees. This pit viper is often found on branches, big leaves, or shrubs in tropical forests. It hangs on with its prehensile tail and strikes at birds, tree frogs, and other animals that come near it. It waits for venom to kill its prey before gulping it down.

Finally, the "pit viper" name tells you that it's in the pit-viper family, which also includes rattlesnakes, cottonmouths, and other venomous species. Pit vipers are named for the pit organ between the nostril and eye on either side of the head. The pit organs sense heat and help a snake aim at its prey when it strikes. Like other vipers, the eyelash palm pit viper has long fangs that spring forward when it bites, as if on hinges.

FAMILY
Viperidae

FACTS

OTHER COMMON NAMES
Eyelash viper, horned palm viper, Schlegel's viper

SCIENTIFIC NAME
Bothriechis schlegelii

SIZE
22–32 inches (56–81 cm)

FOOD
Lizards, frogs, small mammals, birds

HABITAT
Rain forests

RANGE
Central and South America

Eyelash palm pit vipers can also be green, brown, silver, pink, or gray, with speckles and bands of different colors.

GABOON VIPER

FAMILY
Viperidae

FACTS

OTHER COMMON NAMES
Swamp jack, rhinoceros viper, Gaboon adder

SCIENTIFIC NAME
Bitis gabonica

SIZE
4–6.5 feet (1.2–2 m)

FOOD
Small mammals, antelope, birds

HABITAT
Rain forests, tropical woodlands

RANGE
Sub-Saharan Africa

The snake world's longest fangs belong to the Gaboon viper. Big snakes of this venomous species can have fangs measuring up to 1.6 inches (4 cm) long! The Gaboon viper sinks these fangs into prey ranging from birds and rats to antelope and even prickly brush-tailed porcupines.

Brown, gray, purple, and tan markings cover its body in a geometric pattern, as if the snake were crafted by a carpetmaker. The beautiful pattern is eye-catching when the snake is in captivity, but it completely camouflages it when it's curled up among leaves on the forest floor. This species hunts by ambushing prey, waiting quietly for animals to walk past it.

The Gaboon viper weighs up to 18 pounds (8 kg), making it Africa's heaviest viper. Despite its size, however, this snake isn't looking for trouble. Scientists and other people who've accidentally stepped on a well-hidden Gaboon viper report that often it doesn't even react.

However, it can move very quickly, and its bite can be deadly even if the victim is a large person. The snake's triangular head is very broad because it contains huge venom glands. A Gaboon viper produces more venom than any other venomous snake: Its venom glands hold about 0.3 ounces (10 mL) of venom. That's enough to deliver a deadly dose to 30 people.

Like all vipers, the Gaboon viper has fangs that swing forward when the viper strikes. Venom flows through the hollow fangs and is injected into the victim.

A viper can control the amount of venom it releases when it bites.

149

A rattlesnake's rattle is made of hollow segments that are connected a bit like snap-together plastic beads. The segments don't come off when the snake sheds its skin. Instead, a new segment is added. But segments often break off over time, so you can't figure out a rattler's age by counting them.

A rattlesnake hatchling starts life with a one-segment rattle called a button.

WESTERN RATTLE- SNAKE

More than 30 species of rattlesnake slither across the Americas. They're unique among snakes for their tail rattles, which they shake rapidly as a warning. A rattler prefers to remain undetected, so it's usually silent, but it will rattle if an animal is about to step on it. It will also rattle if a predator confronts it. Pay attention to this warning—a rattlesnake is venomous! If the loud rattling is ignored, the snake may bite. It can strike at a distance of at least one-third of its body length.

The western rattlesnake is the most widespread species of rattlesnake in western North America. It's represented by a variety of subspecies that range in color from the dark-skinned Arizona black rattlesnake to the tan Hopi rattlesnake.

Rattlesnakes prey mainly on rodents such as ground squirrels and other small mammals. This diet makes them important allies for farmers, whose crops are favorite meals for ground squirrels. In southern Idaho, U.S.A., scientists discovered that young ground squirrels make up about 80 percent of the western rattler's diet. The snakes were eating about 14 percent of the ground squirrels' young population every year.

FAMILY
Viperidae

FACTS

OTHER COMMON NAMES
Plains rattlesnake, prairie rattlesnake

SCIENTIFIC NAME
Crotalus viridis

SIZE
2–5 feet (0.6–1.5 m)

FOOD
Small mammals, birds, reptiles

HABITAT
Prairies, rocky areas, brush

RANGE
Western North America from southern Canada to northern Mexico

SIDE-WINDER

FAMILY
Viperidae

FACTS

OTHER COMMON NAMES
Horned rattlesnake, sidewinder rattlesnake

SCIENTIFIC NAME
Crotalus cerastes

SIZE
18–32 inches (45–80 cm)

FOOD
Small mammals, birds, reptiles

HABITAT
Sandy deserts

RANGE
Southwestern United States, northwestern Mexico

Wander among the dunes of a desert in the southwestern United States early on a summer morning, and you might spy a series of parallel lines in the sand. The J-shaped lines tilt diagonally, as if someone made check marks across the desert. These mysterious marks are the trail left behind by a sidewinder.

The sidewinder is a species of small rattlesnake the color of desert sand. Like other snakes that live on loose sand in other parts of the world, the sidewinder travels by throwing its body sideways in a looping motion. First one half of the snake touches down and then the other, with the body lifted up in between. The snake looks as if it's gliding across the desert.

Sidewinders spend hot summer days hiding in an abandoned rodent burrow or other shelter. They emerge at night to seek food. Adults feed on a variety of small animals. Newborn sidewinders catch little lizards by wriggling their tails to attract them. The small, young sidewinders are born alive in burrows, where they will stay by day for their first week or two.

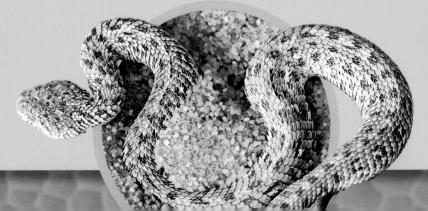

Sidewinders aren't the only sidewinders! Some desert snakes in Africa also sidewind, as do a few Asian water snakes when they travel across slick mudflats.

Hornlike scales stick up above a sidewinder's eyes. They may help prevent sand from covering the snake's eyes when it's buried.

Male adders fight with each other over mates. The snakes don't bite—instead, they try to force each other to the ground.

Some common adders are black. They tend to be found in northern areas, where their dark color lets them soak up sunshine quicker than regular adders.

ADDER

No snake lives farther north than the common adder. This species is the only snake that exists above the Arctic Circle. The Arctic Circle is a line that appears on maps and encircles the treeless far north. The Arctic is home to animals such as polar bears and reindeer that are adapted to life in the cold. It's not a place you'd expect to find snakes.

The adder, however, has evolved behaviors to cope with cold. During winter, for example, an adder hibernates in a den shared with other adders. Hibernation may last as little as five months in some parts of its wide range, but an adder in northern regions can hibernate for as long as nine months. Female adders give live birth in late summer. Just a few weeks later, the hatchlings find a den in which to hibernate.

Adders emerge in spring, even if there's snow on the ground, as long as there is sunshine available for basking. The males wake up from hibernation first. They shed their skins, bask in the sun, and are ready to mate by the time the females emerge from dens a few weeks later. Females, which are bigger than males, are yellowish, brown, or reddish in color. Males are usually a creamy or silvery gray. Both are marked with a dark zigzag stripe running down the back.

FAMILY
Viperidae

FACTS

OTHER COMMON NAMES
Common adder, European adder, common viper, northern viper, crossed viper

SCIENTIFIC NAME
Vipera berus

SIZE
2–3 feet (0.6–1 m)

FOOD
Frogs, lizards, young birds, small mammals

HABITAT
Moors, woodlands, swamps, marshes, meadows, coastal sand dunes

RANGE
Eurasia

155

EASTERN HOG-NOSED SNAKE

And the Academy Award for best actor in the reptile world goes to—the eastern hog-nosed snake! This snake is famous for the displays it puts on when it's attacked by a predator.

First, a hog-nosed snake reacts by puffing up and hissing. It jabs its head as if attempting to bite. If this cobra act doesn't scare off its attacker, the snake goes into its "death" throes. It rolls on its back and writhes vigorously as if it's in terrible pain. It may even throw up its last meal. Finally, it lies still with its mouth gaping open and tongue lolling out, drooling. It won't recover and crawl away until the danger is past.

The hog-nosed snake, as far as humans are concerned, is all bluff and no bite. It rarely bites people; it's more interested in biting toads, its main food. Toads are intimidating meals—many species ooze poison, and they often puff up their bodies when attacked by snakes, which makes them hard to swallow.

But a hog-nosed snake can stretch its jaws around an inflated toad. It also has fangs in the back of its upper jaw that inject venom. The venom is mild and harmless to humans, but deadly to toads. The fangs may also help release air from the blown-up toad, as if popping a balloon. In addition, the hog-nosed snake appears to be immune to the toad's poison.

The hog-nosed snake is named after its upturned snout, which it uses as a shovel to dig burrows and root up toads to eat.

Hog-nosed snakes are famous for "playing dead" in self-defense. This trick is called death feigning. It works because many predators lose interest in prey that's already dead.

When a green vine snake feels threatened, it turns toward its attacker and opens its brightly colored mouth and puffs up its body, which reveals a surprising black-and-white checkerboard pattern.

The green vine snake of Central and South America is a different species that shares a common name as well as a similar habitat and adaptations (see page 41).

GREEN VINE SNAKE

If you guessed that the green vine snake lives among green vines, you're correct! This long, very thin snake winds slowly among the vines, branches, and leaves of its treetop habitat. It relies on camouflage to hide it from predators and prey. If the snake senses danger, it freezes in place so that it looks like nothing more than a vine. But if a wind is rustling the leaves, then the snake will sway slowly so that it, too, appears to be dancing in the breeze.

The green vine snake's skinny shape extends right into its thin, arrow-shaped head. A slender groove runs down each side of its face, right in front of the eye and perfectly lined up with its keyhole-shaped pupil. A green vine snake aims its vision on its prey like a cat focusing on a mouse, judges the distance carefully, and then jabs its head forward to seize it.

This snake is a "rear-fanged" species—it delivers venom with teeth in the back of its mouth, not with fangs in the front of the mouth like vipers. The teeth aren't hollow, like a rattlesnake's fangs; instead, venom runs down grooves in the teeth. After the snake grabs a lizard, it uses its jaws to move the lizard to the back of its mouth so it can sink its rear fangs into its body and kill it with venom.

FACTS

OTHER COMMON NAMES
Long-nosed whip snake

SCIENTIFIC NAME
Ahaetulla nasuta

SIZE
3–5 feet (1–1.5 m)

FOOD
Birds, lizards, frogs

HABITAT
Rain forests, woodlands, swamps

RANGE
South and Southeast Asia

PARADISE FLYING SNAKE

FACTS

OTHER COMMON NAMES
Paradise tree snake, garden
flying snake

SCIENTIFIC NAME
Chrysopelea paradisi

SIZE
3–4 feet (1–1.2 m)

FOOD
Frogs, lizards, small
mammals

HABITAT
Forests

RANGE
Southeast Asia

Most of the time, a paradise flying snake looks like an ordinary snake—a tubular, scaly reptile that can climb a tree and curl around a branch.

But if a predator approaches, the snake does a very surprising thing: It leaps out of the tree and soars through the air!

The paradise flying snake doesn't actually fly. It doesn't have wings. What it does is glide, like the flying dragon (pages 90–91). It lifts its ribs so that its normally sausage-like body flattens out and becomes curved along its underside. This shape change turns its body into a glider that can sail down at an angle to another tree or the ground. The snake can even control the direction of its flight by wiggling its body in S-shapes as it glides. Using this strategy, flying snakes are able to glide up to 100 feet (30 m).

Flying snakes only came to the attention of scientists in the 1800s. At first, scientists didn't believe the local people who told them about the flying snakes. Today, some researchers study how the snakes glide to get ideas for new flying machines. Others are trying to find out if the snakes glide while hunting or simply to travel from tree to tree.

Herpetologists aren't the only scientists researching flying snakes. Physicists, who study such topics as energy, force, and motion, are also interested in the details of how the snakes glide.

A flying snake gets ready for takeoff. First, it hangs from a branch so that it looks like a letter J. Then it swings its body up and forward. Its body flattens and arches as it sails into the air.

The African egg-eater doesn't need venom or sharp teeth to "catch" eggs. As a result, it has no defenses. Instead, it puffs up, hisses, and even makes rasping noises with rough scales on its side to mimic venomous species.

An egg-eating snake examines an egg before eating it to make sure it's a fresh egg that contains only liquid and not a solid baby bird. After swallowing the liquid, the snake throws up the eggshell as a folded-up mass.

AFRICAN EGG-EATING SNAKE

Imagine living on a food that is available only in spring and fasting for the rest of the year.

That describes the life of the African egg-eating snake. Many snakes eat eggs, but they usually just swallow them whole. The egg-eater, however, has evolved adaptations that make it an egg-processing machine!

The snake's meal starts with a raid on a bird's nest either on the ground or in a shrub or tree. It braces an egg against a solid surface as it wraps its jaws around it. The snake's jaws and skin stretch so much that it can engulf an egg that's four times as big as its head.

Things only get more interesting once the egg is in its throat. There, the egg is held in place, pierced, and crushed—not by teeth, but by hard, spiky points on the bottom of some of its vertebrae that stick into, but not through, the snake's throat.

Most of these special vertebrae simply hold the entire egg in its throat and stop it from popping out of its mouth or sliding into its stomach. In between, other vertebrae pierce the egg and crush the shell so that the egg's liquid contents flow into the stomach. Then the broken eggshell is mashed into a clump and thrown up.

FAMILY
Colubridae

FACTS

OTHER COMMON NAMES
Common egg-eater, egg-eating snake, rhombic egg-eater

SCIENTIFIC NAME
Dasypeltis scabra

SIZE
2.5–3 feet (0.8–1 m)

FOOD
Eggs

HABITAT
Many habitats except rain forests and deserts

RANGE
Africa

BOOM-SLANG

FAMILY
Colubridae

FACTS

OTHER COMMON NAMES
Tree snake

SCIENTIFIC NAME
Dispholidus typus

SIZE
4–6 feet (1.2–1.8 m)

FOOD
Birds, lizards

HABITAT
Savanna woodlands, thornbush

RANGE
Sub-Saharan Africa

The boomslang doesn't seem like a terribly threatening snake. It's long and slender, with an appetite for lizards and other small prey. But its venom is extremely strong. One bite is enough to kill a human.

The boomslang, however, isn't aggressive. Most people bitten by this snake have been handling it or trying to harm it. Fortunately, hospitals in boomslang regions have a medicine, called antivenom, that treats the effects of a boomslang bite. (Professional reptile handlers may also have antivenom on hand for emergencies.)

Like other venomous snakes, the boomslang uses its venom to kill prey. This species hunts in trees, sneaking up on chameleons and then suddenly striking. A boomslang's fangs are located toward the back of its mouth. The snake chomps on its wriggling prey to work more venom into its body.

The name "boomslang" means "tree snake" in Afrikaans, a language spoken in some African countries. Boomslangs are very much at home in treetops. They come in a variety of colors that camouflage them among branches and leaves. They even mate in trees, which is very unusual for snakes. Females lay eggs on the ground near trees or in empty birds' nests.

Antivenom is used to fight the harmful effects of venom. It's made by "milking" venom from the fangs of captive snakes. The venom is dried, added to a salty solution, and injected into a horse or sheep. The dose is too small to hurt the animal, but its blood still makes substances to fight the venom. Then small amounts of blood are taken out (again, without harm) and used to make antivenom solutions for people and other animals.

A boomslang has elongated pupils like the green vine snake (pages 158–159), which help it focus on prey and judge the distance to reach it.

Wild corn snakes vary in color from place to place. Their colors include red, orange, brown, and gray.

CORN SNAKE

How did the corn snake get its name? It may be a result of its appetite—not for corn, but for corn-eating pests. Farmers used to store corn in wooden structures called corncribs. Slats in the crib let air circulate around the corn. Unfortunately, rats and mice sneaked in, too. The orange snakes that showed up to feast on these rodents earned both the farmers' gratitude and the name "corn snake."

The corn snake's underside, however, could also have inspired its name. Its belly is a checkerboard of large scales colored mainly black and white. The pattern resembles an ear of multicolored flint corn.

Corn snakes are common in the wild, yet aren't a common sight. In the southern part of their range, for example, they're mainly active at night. They also tend to hide under rocks and logs or in burrows. In spite of their fondness for lying low, corn snakes are actually excellent climbers and will creep up trees to feed on bird eggs, nestlings, and even roosting bats!

Corn snakes are now found outside their natural range in places such as Hawaii, U.S.A.; the Caribbean; and Europe. The snakes reached these places accidentally in ships' cargo or are escaped pets.

FAMILY
Colubridae

FACTS

OTHER COMMON NAMES
Red rat snake, scarlet racer, chicken snake, eastern corn snake

SCIENTIFIC NAME
Pantherophis guttatus

SIZE
2–6 feet (0.6–1.8 m)

FOOD
Lizards, frogs, birds, small mammals

HABITAT
Woodlands, fields, wetlands, pine barrens

RANGE
Eastern and southeastern United States

TENTACLED SNAKE

FACTS

OTHER COMMON NAMES
Fishing snake

SCIENTIFIC NAME
Erpeton tentaculatum

SIZE
2–3 feet (0.6–1 m)

FOOD
Fish

HABITAT
Lakes, ponds, rivers, streams, ditches, rice paddies

RANGE
Southeast Asia

Weird and wonderful—that's the tentacled snake. Its oddity begins at its snout, which is tipped with the two fingerlike tentacles that inspired its name. Then there's the strange way it hangs out in the water: It spends much of its time clinging to an underwater plant or root with its tail and remaining stock-still with its body held in the shape of the letter J.

It turns out the snake's fishhook shape actually helps it hook fish! The snake, camouflaged so that it looks like an innocent stick, is approached by fish. When a fish moseys into the bend of the J near the snake's neck, the snake ripples its neck muscles. This sends a pulse of water toward the fish. Water moving like this means "predator nearby" to a fish, so it turns sharply to zip off in the opposite direction. It doesn't even think about the situation because the zipping-away is a reflex, like the reflex that makes you yank your hand away if you touch a hot stove.

Unfortunately for the fish, this reflex sends it swimming toward the snake's head—and sometimes right into its mouth! The snake simply snaps its head toward the tricked fish to seize it.

The tentacled snake is the only snake with tentacles. The tentacles were once thought to be lures for attracting prey, but they actually help the snake sense fish in murky water or at night.

The tentacled snake stays stiff and still as it waits for prey. It will also remain stiff as a board if a person lifts it out of the water.

Many milk snakes aren't affected by the venom of other snakes.

eggs and hatchlings

SINALOAN MILK SNAKE

The Sinaloan milk snake, like other milk snakes, has a slim, smooth body and a narrow head. It's easy to tell apart from other milk snakes, though, because its red bands are much wider than its black and yellow bands.

Many milk snakes resemble venomous coral snakes. Their colors may function as a warning even though milk snakes aren't venomous. The colorful bands also seem to flicker as a snake slithers swiftly away from a predator. This flickering may make it harder for a predator to track the snake's movement and give it extra time to escape.

But why the name "milk snake"? This name comes from an old legend that milk snakes steal milk from cows! Some farmers in olden times believed this because the snakes were often found in barns. The snakes, however, were there to eat rodents, not to drink milk from cows' udders—something a snake can't physically do.

FAMILY
Colubridae

FACTS

OTHER COMMON NAMES
Milk snake

SCIENTIFIC NAME
Lampropeltis triangulum sinaloae

SIZE
3–4 feet (1–1.2 m)

FOOD
Reptiles, amphibians, small mammals

HABITAT
Rocky, dry areas

RANGE
Northwestern Mexico

Milk snakes kill their prey by constricting. A milk snake holds on to the prey's head while coiling around it. Like other constrictors, a milk snake can sense its prey's heartbeat. It uncoils when the heartbeat stops and swallows its prey headfirst.

MADAGASCAR LEAF-NOSED SNAKE

Madagascar is a Texas-size island that lies off the coast of Africa. It's home to a stunning variety of animals, about three-quarters of which are found nowhere else on Earth. Among these unique creatures is the Madagascar leaf-nosed snake.

You don't usually notice a snake's snout—but you can't miss the one on this species! A male leaf-nosed snake has a long, spearlike point on its snout. The female's snout ends in a wide, leaflike blade. Nobody knows just what these nose projections do for the snakes.

A leaf-nosed snake may hang from a branch to ambush prey. It also waves like a vine in a breeze and slowly stalks unsuspecting lizards. As a result, some herpetologists suggest that the nose structures camouflage the snakes by making them resemble twigs or seedpods. Some scientists suggest that the strange noses may help the snake hone in on the back of its victim's neck, where it often grabs its prey. Why the males and females look so different is also a puzzle!

An old folk belief says that the male snake drops headfirst out of trees to stab animals passing under it with its spearlike nose! The snakes don't really do this—plus, the "spear" is soft and flexible.

A female snake's leafy nose makes her easy to tell apart from the pointy-nosed male. The male and the female also wear different colors.

When a leaf-nosed snake hatches, its nose structure is folded back and stuck to the top of its head. It unfolds into its normal position within the first two days after hatching.

Colors are used in the names of other kinds of garter snakes, too. Examples include the red-spotted garter snake, the blue-striped garter snake, and the blackbelly garter snake.

Tens of thousands of red-sided garter snakes hibernate in limestone caves north of Narcisse, Manitoba, Canada. The nearby town of Inwood features a huge statue of the species.

RED-SIDED GARTER SNAKE

As days warm up in early spring, red-sided garter snakes start emerging from their winter dens in Canada. They lounge around the dens' openings, basking—and waiting. These snakes are all males, and they're waiting for the later-rising females to creep out of the dens.

When they do, a frenzy begins. Each female gives off a special scent signal called a pheromone that attracts males. She is immediately swarmed by dozens of males all vying to mate with her. The males form a giant, writhing ball around the female as they push each other around and try to get closer to her.

In early summer, each female will give birth to 10 to 15 young. When days shorten and temperatures drop in the fall, the snakes will migrate back to the dens. Some may travel for miles. Inside the dens, snakes grow cold and inactive, but they avoid the freezing winter weather that could kill them.

The red-sided garter snake is one of many subspecies of the common garter snake, North America's most widespread snake species. It's the most northerly subspecies. Other subspecies range as far south as Central America.

FAMILY
Colubridae

FACTS

OTHER COMMON NAMES
Garter snake

SCIENTIFIC NAME
Thamnophis sirtalis parietalis

SIZE
1.5–2 feet (0.5–0.6 m)

FOOD
Insects, fish, frogs, salamanders, small mammals

HABITAT
Streams, ponds, lakes, marshes, fields, forest edges, meadows, grasslands, woodlands

RANGE
Central North America

KING COBRA

FAMILY
Elapidae

FACTS

OTHER COMMON NAMES
Hamadryad

SCIENTIFIC NAME
Ophiophagus hannah

SIZE
10–13 feet (3–4 m)

FOOD
Snakes, lizards, eggs, small mammals

HABITAT
Plains, rain forests

RANGE
South and Southeast Asia

The world's largest venomous snake is the king cobra—a reptile that delivers so much venom when it bites that it could kill an elephant.

King cobras can grow to be about 13 feet (4 m) long, though some giants have measured up to 18 feet (5.5 m). When threatened, it will raise the front third of its body off the ground. This position puts it nearly eye to eye with a human. To add to its menacing posture, the snake flares its neck and growls loudly.

Though it is a fierce snake if threatened, the king cobra prefers to mind its own business. It isn't commonly seen in the wild because it's secretive. It also exhibits behavior that, to people, looks like it has a softer side: It's the only snake known to build a nest for its eggs. The female constructs the nest by coiling her body in order to gather leaves, sticks, and soil into a heap. She even guards the nest until her eggs are ready to hatch.

The king cobra's genus name, *Ophiophagus,* means "snake-eater." It specializes in eating other snakes. Its strong venom paralyzes its prey and starts digesting it even as it's being swallowed.

A female king cobra is "king of the hill" when it comes to her nest. She stays coiled on it for the two to three months it takes for the eggs to incubate. She doesn't even leave to find food.

A king cobra spreads the ribs at the back of its neck to make itself look bigger. This behavior is called "hooding."

A bandy-bandy swallows a blind snake headfirst. If it eats a super-long blind snake, it starts digesting the swallowed portion while the extra length hangs out of its mouth.

One hypothesis for the bandy-bandy's dazzling black and white rings is that they make it hard for a predator to pinpoint the snake's exact position when it races away in dim light.

BANDY-BANDY

With its bold black and white markings, a bandy-bandy looks as if it would be a very venomous snake that stalks prey whenever and wherever it wants. But looks can be deceiving! This species is actually quite secretive, and little is known about it.

This mystery is partly due to its habits. For a start, it's nocturnal. Most people only see a bandy-bandy if they drive through its range on a rainy night and spot one crossing the road. In addition, the bandy-bandy is a burrower. It spends most of its time tucked under logs or rocks or hiding underground.

There the bandy-bandy pursues its equally secretive prey: blind snakes. The wormlike blind snakes feed on ant eggs and larvae. Bandy-bandies are thought to feed almost solely on blind snakes. A bandy-bandy can swallow a blind snake that's longer than its own body.

The bandy-bandy is venomous, but its mouth is small and it doesn't often bite in self-defense. Instead, it uses a strange behavior to confuse predators, such as owls and cats. Resting its head and tail on the ground, it holds loops of its body in the air. The weird position combined with the black and white rings make it hard for the predator to figure out which end of the snake is its head, what it's doing, and in which direction it might dash!

FAMILY
Elapidae

FACTS

OTHER COMMON NAMES
Bandy-snake, hoop snake

SCIENTIFIC NAME
Vermicella annulata

SIZE
20–31 inches (50–80 cm)

FOOD
Blind snakes

HABITAT
Deserts, plains, woodlands, rain forests

RANGE
Northern and eastern Australia

BRAHMINY BLIND SNAKE

FAMILY
Typhlopidae

OTHER COMMON NAMES
Flowerpot snake, island blind snake

SCIENTIFIC NAME
Ramphotyphlops braminus

SIZE
2.5–6.5 inches (6–16.5 cm)

FOOD
Ant and termite eggs and young

HABITAT
Moist ground, leaf litter, mulch in urban areas, farmland, forests

RANGE
Africa, Asia, Australia, the Americas, many oceanic islands

If someone told you about a snake that might one day colonize most of the planet, you probably wouldn't picture a tiny wriggler smaller than a shoelace. This world-conquering snake, however, is truly one of the most harmless and smallest species of snake: the Brahminy blind snake.

The Brahminy blind snake lives underground, in piles of damp leaves, under logs, and in other dark places. It feeds on the eggs and young of ants and termites. It doesn't need sharp eyesight in its dark world, so the tiny specks of eyes on its head can only tell light from dark. Its head is barely distinguishable from its tail, which is tipped with a small spur that probably helps it brace itself as it burrows.

Brahminy blind snakes are often mistaken for earthworms. But it's easy to tell them apart. The blind snake has scales, while an earthworm's body has rings, or segments. An earthworm can move by stretching and squashing its body like an accordion, but a blind snake can't.

Being a soil-dwelling animal, the Brahminy blind snake has been able to travel worldwide in the soil of plants being shipped to new countries. This mode of transport has given the species its common name of "flowerpot snake." It is also the only snake species known to be made up entirely of females!

There are no male Brahminy blind snakes! A female Brahminy blind snake lays eggs without mating. They hatch out into sisters that are identical to their mother and to each other.

The Brahminy blind snake sometimes startles people in parts of Asia by climbing up through a bathroom drain! But it's totally harmless. It's not venomous, and it has a very small mouth with just a few tiny teeth inside.

ALL ABOUT
WORM LIZARDS

The third group of animals in the order Squamata is the family of worm lizards—reptiles that look like giant earthworms. They are also called amphisbaenians. There are about 170 species. They're found mainly in Central and South America as well as in much of Africa.

A worm lizard's resemblance to an earthworm is no accident. Both animals have evolved to burrow underground, and their bodies are shaped to do this efficiently. Many people who accidentally dig up a worm lizard think they've found a supersize worm.

But a closer look shows that a worm lizard is covered with scales, like other reptiles. The scales lie in rings around the body. A worm lizard also has an internal skeleton, unlike a worm, as well as a snakelike tongue!

Most worm-lizard species are legless. Legs get in the way of slipping through burrows. A few species, however, have a pair of clawed front legs for digging.

Worm lizards have tiny eyes, hidden beneath scales, that can sense only light and dark. But that's all this reptile needs to see. It relies on its hidden ears and its sensitive tongue to find its prey. It seizes prey with its scissorlike teeth and tears out chunks.

A worm lizard's skin is somewhat loosely connected to its body, as if it were wearing a sock one size too large. This loose skin allows the reptile to stretch and shrink its body as it moves, like an accordion—a useful ability for creeping through tunnels. Many worm lizards can shed their tails, to escape predators. But unlike lizards, worm lizards can lose their tails only once—they can't grow them back.

Short worm lizard
(Pachycalamus brevis)
The short worm lizard is found only on the island of Socotra in the Indian Ocean.

Zarudny's worm lizard
(Diplometopon zarudnyi)
The Zarudny's worm lizard lives throughout the Middle East. Its flattened, scaly head helps it burrow in sand and soil.

Vanzolini's worm lizard
(Amphisbaena vanzolinii)
The Vanzolini's worm lizard is named after a Brazilian zoologist who studied amphisbaenians.

Speckled worm lizard
(Amphisbaena fuliginosa)
Speckled worm lizards live in rain forests of northern South America. Scientists were surprised to find a few living in a dry grassland, too!

RED WORM LIZARD

FAMILY
Amphisbaenidae

FACTS

OTHER COMMON NAMES
White-bellied worm lizard, white worm lizard, giant amphisbaenian

SCIENTIFIC NAME
Amphisbaena alba

SIZE
16–30 inches (42–75 cm)

FOOD
Insects, spiders, worms

HABITAT
Savannas, rain forests, farmland

RANGE
South America

One of the biggest worm lizards in the world is the red worm lizard, which can grow as long as a sidewinder rattlesnake and as big around as a jumbo ballpark frankfurter! Unlike a rattlesnake, however (or a hot dog), the red worm lizard spends most of its life burrowing underground. It sometimes comes to the surface, where it's likely to hide in leaf litter.

Red worm lizards usually feed on small prey such as ants and other insects as well as spiders. They are known to live in the nests of leaf-cutter ants and don't appear to be bothered by the ants' bites and stings. Captive red worm lizards have revealed that their jaws are strong enough to tackle meals such as mice.

A red worm lizard that feels threatened defends itself by curling up and raising its head and tail. This behavior has led people to call it "the two-headed snake" because the back and front ends look so much alike—that is, until the worm lizard opens its jaws!

The red worm lizard's body is also covered in tough skin, with particularly strong fibers in its tail. Snakes, however, can overcome this armor and are major predators of worm lizards.

In 2009, scientists published a paper reporting the sighting of a red worm lizard swimming in a river. Until then, it was thought that worm lizards couldn't easily travel to new habitats.

A red worm lizard's nostrils open to the side and back so that they don't get filled with dirt, as they would if they faced forward.

185

The European worm lizard is also known as the Mediterranean or Iberian worm lizard. It is eaten by snakes, skinks, centipedes, and even wild boars. A worm lizard is quick to start burrowing to escape a predator.

European worm lizards mate in late winter. Scented fluids released from their hind ends may help the reptiles find each other.

EUROPEAN WORM LIZARD

The European worm lizard was one of the first worm-lizard species to be studied closely.

Scientists have turned over stones, rolled logs to the side, and dug into the soil to find out more about this burrowing animal. Today, they also use advanced technology that's powerful enough to see what's hiding inside a rock!

In 2011, a researcher who was studying fossils found an interesting rock in Spain. He knew it contained a fossil, but he feared it would be ruined if anybody chipped away at the rock. So scientists used a CT scanner to peer inside the rock instead.

Usually, fossils are found in bits and pieces and must be put together like a puzzle. But the CT scanner revealed a nearly complete, tiny skull hiding inside the rock. It belonged to an ancestor of the European worm lizard that lived about 11 million years ago. The discovery showed that worm lizards haven't changed much in a very long time.

Scientists are also learning more about the European worm lizard. For example, research shows that worm lizards in southwestern areas of its range show genetic differences that might mean they're a separate species. These worm lizards are a bit larger and have a different number of rings on their bodies.

FAMILY
Blanidae

FACTS

OTHER COMMON NAMES
Mediterranean worm lizard, Iberian worm lizard, blind snake

SCIENTIFIC NAME
Blanus cinereus

SIZE
4–8 inches (10–20 cm)

FOOD
Ants, ant larvae, termites

HABITAT
Moist, sandy soils

RANGE
Portugal, Spain

FLORIDA WORM LIZARD

FACTS

OTHER COMMON NAMES
Graveyard snake, thunder worm

SCIENTIFIC NAME
Rhineura floridana

SIZE
7–12 inches (18–30 cm)

FOOD
Worms, termites, spiders

HABITAT
Sandy soils

RANGE
Northern and central Florida; small area in Georgia, U.S.A.

Sandy soil is home, sweet home for the Florida worm lizard. This species is the only living one in its family. It's also the only worm lizard in the United States. Other species, long extinct, once burrowed through the soil of the country's plains. Now only their fossils remain.

With its pale pink coloring, the Florida worm lizard looks even more wormlike than other species. It burrows in compost and leaf litter aboveground. If it's disturbed, however, it quickly dives back into a tunnel—tail first!

The shovel-like head of the Florida worm lizard resembles the upturned snout of the eastern hog-nosed snake (pages 156–157). These two reptiles aren't cousins; fossil and genetic clues show that worm lizards seem to be closely related to certain lizards, not snakes. But they have both evolved adaptations that help them burrow—an example of convergent evolution.

This species' nickname of "graveyard snake" sounds spooky, but it's simply based on the fact that worm lizards often pop up when people dig in the ground. Like Brahminy blind snakes (pages 180–181), worm lizards also make surprise appearances in gardens, and hungry birds are quick to pounce on them.

Florida worm lizards often appear aboveground after a heavy rainstorm, which is why some people call them "thunder worms."

The Florida worm lizard's spadelike head helps it burrow. It digs by shoving its head into the soil and then moving its head up and down to bore a tunnel and clear dirt out of the way.

189

Mexico is also home to three-toed and four-toed species of ajolotes.

The ajolote is often called a mole lizard because its clawed feet look like a mole's. Both animals dig tunnels underground and live mainly out of sight.

AJOLOTE

Worm lizards are unusual creatures, and the ajolote may be one of the most unusual among them. Unlike nearly all other species of worm lizard, the ajolote is equipped with a pair of legs close to its head. They aren't merely "leftover" limbs without a function: They are strong, sturdy legs tipped with five claws and used for digging.

The ajolote's name comes from the language spoken by the Aztec people of Mexico. The Aztec ruled over a large kingdom up until about 500 years ago. The word "ajolote" comes from the name of an Aztec god, Xolotl, a name often translated as "monster" or "dog." (It shares this name with a salamander known as both "ajolote" and "axolotl.") In some places, the ajolote is called by a name that means "the little snake with tiny hands."

An ajolote eats small prey it finds in its tunnels. It also creeps close to the surface to sense vibrations made by the footsteps of prey. Then it lunges out of the soil, grabs the prey, and pulls it underground. Ajolotes are also known to gather close to old fence posts that are rotting at their bases. There they feast on the termites eating the rotten wood.

FAMILY
Bipedidae

OTHER COMMON NAMES
Mole lizard, five-toed worm lizard

SCIENTIFIC NAME
Bipes biporus

SIZE
7–9.4 inches (18–24 cm)

FOOD
Ants, termites, insects, larvae, earthworms, small reptiles

HABITAT
Dry lands, deserts

RANGE
Baja California

FACTS

CHECKERBOARD WORM LIZARD

The checkerboard worm lizard is named for the dark and pale scales scattered on its body.
This is one worm lizard that would never be mistaken for a worm!

The checkerboard worm lizard has a special way of drilling through soil. First, it uses the edges of its face to carve into the soil, twisting its head around much like a tunnel-digging machine. It also moves its head from side to side, which packs the soil against the walls of the tunnel. In this way, the worm lizard relentlessly burrows through the ground. It's also often found under rocks.

Little is known about worm lizards, but the checkerboard worm lizard has starred in a few studies looking at worm-lizard life. In one project, researchers noticed that male and female checkerboard worm lizards were often found as pairs under rocks in springtime. Sometimes they found a female sharing the space with young worm lizards. This discovery sparked lots of questions about worm lizards and possible parenting behavior—just one question among many about these mysterious reptiles!

Checkerboard worm lizards are among the few worm lizards that give live birth.

Like the checkerboard worm lizard, the speckled worm lizard of South America is boldly patterned. As juveniles, however, they're blue with black markings!

TURTLES & TORTOISES

ALL ABOUT TURTLES

The ancestors of today's turtles existed early enough in Earth's history to hang out with the first dinosaurs!

Fossil finds show that turtles have been around for about 220 million years. Their evolutionary history is still being figured out by scientists, based on studies of fossils and modern-day reptiles. Recent research suggests that turtles are more closely related to birds and crocodiles than they are to squamates (the group that includes all lizards, snakes, and worm lizards).

Turtles form the second largest order of reptiles, Testudines (also known as Chelonia). There are about 330 species of turtles. They are the only animals with pelvic and shoulder bones inside their rib cages. The ribs, backbone, and plates of bone are fused together to form the shell. The shell itself is made up of three parts: the carapace on top, the plastron on the bottom, and the bridge joining the two together.

The shell is covered with scutes topped with keratin—the material in your fingernails—though some turtles have leathery coverings instead. The shell is armor, but a turtle can feel pain and pressure through it.

Because a turtle's ribs are fused to the carapace, they can't spread to let the turtle breathe in and out. Instead, a turtle uses special muscles.

Like squamates, turtles have scales and a cloaca. They don't have teeth. They don't have external ears, but they do have inner-ear organs and can hear very well. Like most lizards, turtles have movable eyelids. Turtles can only lay eggs—they don't give live birth.

The turtle family includes animals called tortoises and terrapins. What's the difference between them? A "turtle" has webbed feet and spends most of its time in the water. A "tortoise" has stumpy feet for walking on land and doesn't live in water. A "terrapin" dwells both on land and in water and never lives far from a water source.

Ornate box turtle
(Terrapene ornata)
The ornate box turtle is one of just two species of land turtles that lives on the Great Plains of the United States.

Olive ridley sea turtle
(Lepidochelys olivacea)
Olive ridley sea turtles travel hundreds, sometimes thousands, of miles across oceans to beaches where they lay eggs.

Loggerhead turtle
(Caretta caretta)
A loggerhead turtle's sharp, powerful jaws can crunch open the shells of prey such as crabs and conches.

Roti Island snake-necked turtle
(Chelodina mccordi)
The Roti Island snake-necked turtle is a rare species that lives in the wild, only on Rote Island in Indonesia.

Yellow-footed tortoise
(Chelonoidis denticulata)
The yellow-footed tortoise lives in rain forests in South America.

Florida softshell turtle
(Apalone ferox)
A young Florida softshell turtle peeks out from under the edge of its leathery shell.

BOX TURTLE

FAMILY
Emydidae

FACTS

OTHER COMMON NAMES
Eastern box turtle,
common box turtle

SCIENTIFIC NAME
Terrapene carolina

SIZE
4–8.5 inches (10–21.6 cm)

FOOD
Worms, insects, slugs,
snails, fruit, mushrooms,
flowers, eggs, salamanders,
frogs, fish, snakes, carrion

HABITAT
Open woodlands, meadows,
floodplains, pastures,
marshlands

RANGE
Eastern North America

The box turtle is named for its ability to shut its shell as if sealing itself inside a box. Its plastron is hinged, like a door, which allows the turtle to slam itself almost completely closed with its legs, tail, and head tucked safely inside.

The box turtle is a terrestrial turtle, which means it lives on land and not in the water. But the kind of land it favors is damp, and it likes to plop into water for a swim. Box turtles are most active after it rains. They are out and about during the day, looking for food, and basking in the sun. On hot days, they retreat to moist, cool places under logs, among leaves, in mud, or in burrows.

Cold northern winters send box turtles into hibernation. They burrow into mud, soil, or even the bottoms of streams. Turtles in warmer southern locations don't hibernate. In spring, the female digs a nest chamber in which to lay her eggs. Hatchlings have many predators, but those that reach adulthood are well protected by their shells and can live up to 100 years!

The common box turtle includes several subspecies. The eastern or common box turtle has the largest range; in the United States, you can bump into it from Maine all the way down south to Tennessee and Georgia and into the Midwest as far as Michigan.

Most male box turtles have red eyes. A female has golden-brown eyes.

Box turtles can eat mushrooms that are poisonous to humans.

199

Black-knobbed map turtles live in rivers and streams that ultimately drain into Mobile Bay. Mobile Bay is a body of water in southern Alabama that is connected to the Gulf of Mexico.

Black-knobbed map turtles often feed while underwater. Among their foods are bryozoans—tiny, simple animals that clump together in colonies that look like mossy blobs.

People have also preyed on these turtles, mainly for the pet trade. Today, the turtles are protected by law in some places.

BLACK-KNOBBED MAP TURTLE

The black-knobbed map turtle is named after the black-tipped spikes that run down its back. It's also known as a "sawback." The "map" in the name refers to the wavy lines on its body, which look like markings on a map. This striking turtle could just as easily have been named after the jagged edges of its carapace, which make it look like a child's drawing of the sun.

A perfect waterway for these turtles is one that offers lots of basking sites as well as currents that are neither too swift nor too slow. Black-knobbed map turtles like to perch on logs, riverside shrubs, or bunches of plants sticking out of the water in order to soak up the sun. They prefer basking sites that give them a clear view of their surroundings so they can watch out for predators, such as alligators.

Female black-knobbed map turtles are bigger than males. In late spring and summer, they dig nests in sandy areas near the water and lay their eggs at night. Raccoons, armadillos, and fish crows eagerly eat some eggs. Eggs are also consumed by non-native fire ants, which were accidentally imported in the 1930s as stowaways on cargo ships arriving from South America. Hatchlings, in turn, face predators such as bullfrogs, fish, and birds.

FAMILY
Emydidae

FACTS

OTHER COMMON NAMES
Black-knobbed sawback, delta map turtle

SCIENTIFIC NAME
Graptemys nigrinoda

SIZE
3–7.5 inches (7.5–19 cm)

FOOD
Insects, sponges, slugs, snails, algae

HABITAT
Streams, rivers

RANGE
Alabama and Mississippi, U.S.A.

HERMANN'S TORTOISE

FAMILY
Testudinidae

OTHER COMMON NAMES
Mediterranean tortoise

SCIENTIFIC NAME
Testudo hermanni

SIZE
5–9 inches (12–23 cm)

FOOD
Flowers, grass, leaves, insects, slugs, snails, worms, carrion

HABITAT
Forests, dry grasslands, scrublands, dry meadows, rocky slopes

RANGE
Southern Europe

FACTS

Many turtles like wet habitats, but the Hermann's tortoise is most at home in a dry one. It's content as long as there are plants to eat, warm places to bask, shady spots for cooling off, and suitable ground for digging nests.

In late fall, this tortoise digs out a burrow beneath a rotting log, a shrub, or other protected place. It tucks itself in among fallen leaves and spends winter in a dormant state. In spring, the tortoise emerges and immediately begins looking for a mate. A male tortoise's courtship behavior involves biting the female and bashing into her sides like a miniature tank!

A female tortoise lays her eggs in a burrow. When her job is done, she trundles off. The eggs hatch about three months later. The hatchlings, small in size and soft shelled, are easy pickings for predators such as birds, rats, foxes, hedgehogs, badgers, snakes, and even wild boars. Out of every thousand hatchlings, only about five will make it to the age of three years.

The Hermann's tortoise is a threatened species due to habitat loss and past collection for the pet trade.

Hermann's tortoises and other species are being helped by an organization called SOPTOM, which in French stands for "Station for the Observation and Protection of Turtles and Their Habitats." SOPTOM has special zoos called Turtle Villages where people learn about turtle conservation.

The Hermann's tortoise is named after French doctor and natural-history student Johann Hermann (1738–1800). You can visit his collection of plants, animal skeletons, and other items at the Zoological Museum of Strasbourg, France.

Female Indian star tortoises lay several clutches of eggs each year. The hatchlings' shells have markings that look like spots or butterflies. Star patterns and bumps develop as they grow.

Another starry, bumpy tortoise, the Burmese star tortoise, is found only in Myanmar. It is nearly extinct in the wild, but efforts are being made to save the species by releasing captive-bred turtles.

INDIAN STAR TORTOISE

Bright yellow stars spangle the shell of an Indian star tortoise. Each star sits on one of the peaks rising from the carapace. This beautiful shell is eye-catching to a human, but in the tortoise's natural habitat it works as camouflage. The peaks on the shell are also thought to help the turtle roll over and onto its feet if it happens to fall on its back. Not all star tortoises develop peaks, however.

Unfortunately, the shell that is a life preserver for the tortoise is also the reason it's become endangered. Star tortoises are stolen from the wild and smuggled overseas to sell in the pet trade. It's estimated that 10,000 to 20,000 star tortoises are taken from the wild in India each year. Thousands more are taken to be sold as food. Add habitat loss to the mix, and the future starts to look worrisome for this species.

The star tortoise is protected by laws that make it illegal to collect, sell, or ship them. Authorities rescue hundreds of smuggled tortoises each year. Education and better law enforcement will help a lot in getting star tortoises back on their feet in the wild.

FAMILY
Testudinidae

FACTS

OTHER COMMON NAMES
Sri Lankan star tortoise

SCIENTIFIC NAME
Geochelone elegans

SIZE
6–12 inches (15–30 cm)

FOOD
Leaves, grass, fruit, flowers, insects, worms

HABITAT
Dry areas, semi-deserts, dry grasslands, scrub forests

RANGE
India, Sri Lanka, Pakistan

PANCAKE TORTOISE

FACTS

OTHER COMMON NAMES
Crevice tortoise, softshell tortoise, Tornier's tortoise

SCIENTIFIC NAME
Malacochersus tornieri

SIZE
4–7 inches (10–18 cm)

FOOD
Grass, leaves, flowers, fruit

HABITAT
Dry savannas, scrublands, rocky areas

RANGE
Kenya, Tanzania

Flat as a pancake! That's the pancake tortoise, whose flat shell is unlike that of any other turtle. Its shelled body is only about 1 to 2 inches (2.5–5 cm) thick. It's not only flat, but soft. The edges of the shell are tough and flexible, but the only bony material in the carapace lies under its seams. Scientists who studied this turtle in the late 1800s thought it suffered from a bone disease!

The soft, flat shell's purpose becomes clear when the tortoise escapes from danger. It wedges itself into a narrow crevice between rocks. The flat shell slips neatly into the crevice, and because it's soft, it can also mold itself to the space. It was once thought that the pancake turtle puffed itself up with air like a chuckwalla (pages 72–73) to wedge itself in even more tightly, but it doesn't. Sometimes a crevice may be stuffed with as many as ten turtles.

The squashed body shape means the female doesn't have a lot of room for eggs, so she lays just one egg, or sometimes two, at a time. Pancake tortoises avoid sunlight and heat in their hot habitat, and the female is careful to find a nest site that's the right temperature by testing the ground with her chin.

Like other interesting-looking turtles, the pancake tortoise is declining in the wild due to being collected for the pet trade, even though it's protected by law.

A pancake-tortoise hatchling has a rounded, brightly patterned carapace. It becomes flatter and duller as the tortoise grows.

Pancake tortoises can zip along at a speed of about 59 feet (18 m) per minute. Long claws on their hind feet help them climb rocky outcroppings.

Some Galápagos giant tortoises have shells with an arch in the front. These "saddleback" tortoises can stretch their necks higher to get at food that would otherwise be out of reach. They're found in dry habitats where there are fewer low-growing plants.

Galápagos tortoises are visited by finches, which pick insects and other pests off their bodies.

GALÁPAGOS GIANT TORTOISE

The world's largest land-dwelling turtle, the Galápagos giant tortoise, lives only on a chain of volcanic islands that sit in the Pacific Ocean about 600 miles (966 km) west of the coast of Ecuador. Scientists estimate that tortoises have lived on the Galápagos Islands for about 3 million years. Their ancestors probably drifted there from South America on ocean currents.

Male giant tortoises are typically bigger than females. Very large males have been known to reach 6 feet (1.8 m) in length! Males can weigh from 600 to 700 pounds (272–318 kg). Females weigh from 300 to 400 pounds (136–181 kg). The tortoises walk on sturdy, stumpy legs that look like those of an elephant.

Rain, puddles, and dew licked from rocks provide the tortoises with freshwater. They get moisture from their food, too. The tortoises also travel from feeding areas to pools and springs, following paths carved out by generations of their species over thousands of years.

In the past, sailors on ocean voyages and settlers on the islands used the tortoises for food. The giant tortoises have been protected by law since 1936, and the Galápagos National Park was created in 1959 to conserve this remote habitat and its unique animals.

FAMILY
Testudinidae

FACTS

OTHER COMMON NAMES
Galápagos tortoise, "Galap"

SCIENTIFIC NAME
Chelonoidis nigra

SIZE
2.5–6 feet (0.8–1.8 m)

FOOD
Cactus, grass, leaves, fruit, lichen

HABITAT
Rocky, volcanic island landscapes with grasses, cacti, shrubs

RANGE
Galápagos Islands

ALLIGATOR SNAPPING TURTLE

FAMILY
Chelydridae

FACTS

OTHER COMMON NAMES
Loggerhead turtle, alligator turtle, snapper

SCIENTIFIC NAME
Macrochelys temminckii

SIZE
16–31 inches (40–80 cm)

FOOD
Fish, frogs, snakes, other turtles, snails, worms, clams, crayfish

HABITAT
Rivers, ditches, lakes, swamps

RANGE
Parts of southeastern and central United States

The alligator snapping turtle is North America's biggest freshwater turtle and among the largest in the world. One of the heaviest alligator snapping turtles officially recorded weighed in at a whopping 220 pounds (99.5 kg)! But this turtle isn't remarkable for size alone. It also looks like a science-fiction creature. Spikes jut from its shell. Its large head is equipped with massive jaws tipped with sharp hooks. These jaws are strong enough to bite off a careless person's finger.

The alligator snapping turtle, however, only bites in self-defense or to snap up fish and other prey. It spends most of its time lying still in the water—so still that algae can grow all over it as if it were a rock. It lures curious fish right into its mouth by wiggling a pink, wormlike "sausage" on its tongue. The alligator snapping turtle is the only turtle to use this trick.

A snapper rarely leaves the water. It can stay submerged for about 50 minutes before coming up for a gulp of air. Females climb onto land to lay their eggs in nests close to shore. Raccoons may eat the eggs, and hatchlings are preyed on by birds and fish, but adult snappers have no predators other than humans, who catch them for their meat, their shells, or the pet trade. These tough turtles are declining in some areas. In some states, they're now protected by law.

Scientists recently discovered that there are actually three species of alligator snapping turtle. The two new species live in two different river systems in parts of the southeastern United States. They are not as widespread as *Macrochelys temminckii,* the species shown here.

Alligator snapping turtles have jaws strong enough to bite a broom handle in two. They mainly eat fish and other water creatures, but they're capable of grabbing and eating small mammals and ducks.

A Chinese softshell turtle lays her round eggs in damp soil. The hatchlings pop out about two months later. Scientists who studied the eggs of this species discovered that baby turtles can move toward a source of heat even while they're still developing in their eggs.

Millions of Chinese softshell turtles are raised every year on turtle farms for use as food.

CHINESE SOFTSHELL TURTLE

As you might guess from its name, a softshell turtle's shell isn't hard and bony. Its carapace and plastron are covered with a leathery skin instead of hard, tough scutes. The lack of a hard shell doesn't make this turtle defenseless, however. It can bite hard, and its long, flexible neck allows it to reach backward to nip a person who picks it up.

The Chinese softshell uses its piglike snout as a snorkel so it can remain submerged in water with just its nostrils sticking above the surface. Its feet are heavily webbed to aid in swimming. Another adaptation it has for life underwater is the ability to absorb oxygen from the water through the skin. It pumps water in and out of both its mouth and cloaca to take in oxygen.

Recently, scientists discovered yet another adaptation used by Chinese softshells: the ability to get rid of waste products in their blood by excreting them from the mouth. Digesting proteins in food leaves an oversupply of nitrogen in the body, which the turtle gets rid of by turning it into a substance called urea.

Your body expels urea by using water to flush it out in the form of urine. The Chinese softshell urinates, too, but it often lives in brackish water, so it can't afford to waste water by making lots of urine. Instead, the turtle excretes urea from the mouth's lining and swishes water in and out of its mouth to wash it away.

FAMILY
Trionychidae

FACTS

OTHER COMMON NAMES
None

SCIENTIFIC NAME
Pelodiscus sinensis

SIZE
6–12 inches (15–30 cm)

FOOD
Insects, worms, fish, crustaceans, leaves, seeds

HABITAT
Lakes, rivers, swamps, canals, marshes, ponds, rice paddies

RANGE
China, Japan, Vietnam, Taiwan, Korean Peninsula, Indonesia; introduced to Hawaii, Philippines, Thailand

EASTERN MUSK TURTLE

FAMILY
Kinosternidae

One of the world's smallest turtles is also one of its stinkiest! The eastern musk turtle has glands under the edges of its carapace that produce a terrible-smelling musk when the turtle is upset. This ability has earned it the widely used name of "stinkpot." If the stinky odor fails to keep a predator at bay, this little turtle will also scratch and bite.

The musk turtle spends most of its time in the water, walking on the bottom to look for food. Its long neck helps it reach down for food and also to lift its head out of the water to breathe. Even though it's a water turtle, it's a surprisingly good climber. It can climb onto a log or a floating raft of plant material, and it's even been observed climbing on bushes and low tree branches near the water.

In the warmer parts of its range, the musk turtle is active year-round. It hibernates for the winter in northern areas in a burrow under a rock or log. Dozens of turtles may den together in a larger nook. A musk turtle might also hibernate by burying itself in mud underwater. It can survive thanks to the tiny bumps on its tongue and throat that absorb oxygen from the water. The turtle pulses its throat to make water flow over these body parts.

FACTS

OTHER COMMON NAMES
Stinking Jim, stinkpot, common musk turtle

SCIENTIFIC NAME
Sternotherus odoratus

SIZE
3–5.5 inches (7.6–14 cm)

FOOD
Worms, insects, snails, clams, crayfish, crabs, algae, carrion

HABITAT
Shallow lakes, streams, ponds, rivers, creeks, marshes, swamps, ditches

RANGE
Eastern and midwestern United States, southeastern Canada

Another North American species, the flattened musk turtle, has a shell that's so flat it looks as if it's been run over by a car.

A musk-turtle hatchling's shell is barely an inch (2.5 cm) long. A hatchling could just about perch on a dime.

215

A baby snake-necked turtle's shell is about an inch (2.5 cm) across when it hatches. Hatchlings immediately scramble out of their nest in the sand and head for water. They hide among water plants and eat small fish, insects, and other little animals.

A snake-necked turtle can ooze a foul-smelling fluid in self-defense, a habit that's earned it the nickname "stinker."

EASTERN SNAKE-NECKED TURTLE

Snake-necked turtles are the giraffes of the turtle world. This species has a neck that stretches about half as long as its carapace. Other snake-necked species have even longer necks. The neck of the oblong turtle, for example, can be longer than its carapace, making it look like a snake in a turtle costume.

The eastern snake-necked turtle lives up to its serpentine name when it hunts. Like a snake, it jabs swiftly with its head to strike at its prey. Unlike a snake, the turtle can use its claws to help tear its food into smaller pieces.

How does this turtle manage to pull its head into its shell? It can't pull in its head directly, like a box turtle can. Instead, it bends its neck sideways and tucks its head between its carapace and plastron, like a bird curving its neck to tuck its head underneath a wing. Turtles that pull in their heads this way are known as side-neck turtles.

The eastern snake-necked turtle is usually hidden among water plants. Hot summer days may send it burrowing into the mud of its watery home. During a long-lasting drought, however, snake-necked turtles leave their dried-up bodies of water and head for larger rivers. They will walk very long distances to reach their goal.

FAMILY
Chelidae

FACTS

OTHER COMMON NAMES
Australian snake-necked turtle, eastern long-necked turtle, stinker

SCIENTIFIC NAME
Chelodina longicollis

SIZE
8–10 inches (20–25 cm)

FOOD
Tadpoles, frogs, insects, fish, worms, crustaceans, carrion, zooplankton

HABITAT
Wetlands, rivers, ponds, lagoons

RANGE
Eastern and southeastern Australia

MATAMATA

FAMILY
Chelidae

OTHER COMMON NAMES
Caripatua, mata, matamata turtle

SCIENTIFIC NAME
Chelus fimbriatus

SIZE
12–18 inches (30–45 cm)

FOOD
Fish, aquatic invertebrates

HABITAT
Lakes, ponds, swamps, marshes, rivers, streams

RANGE
Northern South America

FACTS

Picture a bumpy pancake crossed with a piglet, and you've got the matamata! Its flattened carapace is covered with ridges. Its flat, wide head and neck are edged with fringes and flaps. Algae often grow on its shell.

These features add up to perfect camouflage for the matamata, which lives in shallow, muddy water. It lies on the bottom of the water, looking like an algae-covered rock, a mossy branch, or a clump of leaves. Every now and then it sticks its trunklike nose above the surface to breathe. It can also hold its breath for hours and breathe through the lining of its throat and cloaca instead.

Hidden in plain sight, the matamata waits for unsuspecting fish to swim closer. Then it makes its move. It quickly opens its huge mouth so that water rushes into its throat, pulling the fish along with it. The whole process unfolds in less than a second. The matamata then abruptly shuts its mouth, squeezes out the water, and swallows its prey.

The matamata is not only a weird-looking animal, it also smells terrible. It makes a stinky musk that is said to smell like a mixture of urine and dead fish. The awful scent helps to repel predators.

The matamata is known in some places as "the smiling turtle" because its mouth is shaped like a grin.

Matamata hatchlings often sport shades of pink and orange.

These hatchlings are Mary River turtles. The Mary River turtle is an endangered Australian species and is named after the only river in which it lives. Like the Fitzroy River turtle, it can breathe with its cloaca.

A Fitzroy River turtle has bumps called tubercles on its neck. Their purpose is not yet known. One hypothesis is that they are sensitive to touch and vibrations, like a seal's whiskers or an insect's antennae.

FITZROY RIVER TURTLE

TURTLES
Fitzroy River Turtle

The Fitzroy River turtle is one of Australia's most unusual turtles, but it was completely unknown to scientists until the 1970s. Today, it's among the country's best known reptiles even though it's only found in one small part of eastern Australia. Its fame is due largely to its remarkable ability to obtain most of its oxygen by breathing through the skin of the throat or the cloaca (opening in hind end) while underwater.

Turtles have lungs and use them for breathing, but many species are also able to absorb oxygen through the skin of their throats or cloacas while underwater. The Fitzroy River turtle, however, takes this ability to an extreme. Scientists have reported that although they've sometimes seen captive turtles poke their heads out of the water to take a breath, they've never observed Fitzroys doing this in the wild. One wild turtle was recorded as diving into the water and not reappearing for 21 days!

For this species, hind-end breathing appears to be the main way in which it obtains oxygen. It actively takes 15 to 60 "breaths" with its cloaca per minute. It's able to spend hours tucked next to a log or rock in fast-flowing water without budging. When it wants to look for food, it marches across the riverbed with the help of its long forelegs and claws.

Goanna lizards and water rats prey on the turtles' eggs. Non-native animals such as cats, dogs, pigs, and foxes have joined the feast, which poses a threat to the turtles' existence. Volunteers who live near the Fitzroy River work to protect the turtles' nests by installing mesh barriers to keep the eggs away from predators.

FAMILY
Chelidae

FACTS

OTHER COMMON NAMES
Fitzroy tortoise, Fitzroy turtle, bum-breathing turtle, white-eyed river diver

SCIENTIFIC NAME
Rheodytes leukops

SIZE
Up to 10 inches (25 cm)

FOOD
Insects, insect larvae, plant material, algae, sponges, snails

HABITAT
Rivers, streams

RANGE
Queensland, Australia

BIG-HEADED TURTLE

FAMILY
Platysternidae

FACTS

OTHER COMMON NAMES
None

SCIENTIFIC NAME
Platysternon megacephalum

SIZE
6–8 inches (15–20 cm)

FOOD
Worms, snails, crabs, shrimp, fish, frogs, tadpoles

HABITAT
Shallow, rocky mountain streams, in rapidly flowing water or near waterfalls

RANGE
China, Laos, Myanmar, Thailand, Vietnam

One look at this reptile, and you'll know why it's called the big-headed turtle! Its head is nearly half as wide as its carapace. It's so big, the turtle can't pull its head into its shell or even tuck it in sideways like a side-neck species.

Even though a big-headed turtle can't hide its head in its shell, it is still well protected. Its head is shielded by a single big scute that covers the top and reaches down the sides, making the turtle look as if it's wearing a football helmet. It also has hooked jaws and will bite fiercely if bothered. As if that's not enough, it also squeaks loudly and produces a bad-smelling musk.

The big-headed turtle lives in water but is a poor swimmer. Its feet aren't webbed for paddling, but its legs and claws are strong so it can walk on the beds of rocky, shallow streams. It can use its big head and sturdy jaws like a hook to help pull itself over rocks both in water and on land. The turtle also has a muscular tail that's almost as long as its carapace. It uses its tail as a prop as it climbs, too.

Big-headed turtles are such good climbers, they're able to climb bushes and streamside trees. In captivity, they've been known to climb over fences.

In 2013, five big-headed turtles hatched at the Prospect Park Zoo in New York. This success was a first for a zoo belonging to the Association of Zoos and Aquariums, an organization of zoos and aquariums that meet high standards for animal care. Captive breeding is part of the effort to save this endangered species.

A baby big-headed turtle is more brightly colored than an adult. Its tail is also longer in proportion to its body. A big-headed turtle tucks its long tail under the edge of its shell if it feels threatened.

The extra-pointy shells of baby spiny turtles may help protect them from being eaten by snakes and birds. A predator might choose to leave the turtles alone and find something less sharp to swallow!

This baby spiny turtle was hatched in captivity. Spiny turtles are endangered in the wild and hard to breed in captivity. So it was big news when the first hatching of a spiny turtle in Europe occurred in 2004. The turtle hatched at the Durrell Wildlife Park on the island of Jersey in the English Channel.

SPINY TURTLE

The spiny turtle is like a walking circular-saw blade. Sharp spikes stick out from the rim of its carapace. Younger turtles have sharper spikes, because the edges of the carapace wear down as the turtle ages. Old turtles may have almost completely smooth shells with just a few spikes at the back of the carapace. The spines help protect the turtle from predators such as snakes—a big danger for younger, smaller turtles.

A spiny turtle's orange and brown coloring camouflages it on the forest floor, where it hides among fallen leaves. The spines may also help conceal it because they break up the turtle's shape and look like leaf edges.

In the wild, the spiny turtle's breeding season is linked to the rainy season. In captivity, males will not seek out females unless they are first sprayed with water. The female lays no more than three eggs, which are large for her size. Each one is about 2.4 inches (6 cm) long. Her plastron has a hinge in it that enables it to flex while she lays her eggs.

FAMILY
Geoemydidae

FACTS

OTHER COMMON NAMES
Spiny terrapin, spiny hill turtle, sunburst turtle, cogwheel turtle

SCIENTIFIC NAME
Heosemys spinosa

SIZE
7–9 inches (17.5–22 cm)

FOOD
Plants, fruit, insects, worms

HABITAT
Near or in shallow mountain streams in woodlands

RANGE
Southeast Asia

GREEN SEA TURTLE

FACTS

OTHER COMMON NAMES
Green turtle, greenback turtle

SCIENTIFIC NAME
Chelonia mydas

SIZE
3–5 feet (1–1.5 m)

FOOD
Algae, sea grass

HABITAT
Oceans and coastal areas

RANGE
Worldwide in tropical and subtropical waters

You might think the green sea turtle is named for the color of its skin or shell, but it's actually named after the green fat inside its body!

Green sea turtles are endangered, and there are many reasons why. This turtle has long been collected by humans for food. In some places, people eat the turtles' eggs. Turtles also drown in fishing nets. Today, many countries are working together to conserve this endangered species. It needs international cooperation because it lives along the coasts of more than 140 countries and nests on the beaches of more than 80 countries.

Green sea turtles are known for their long-distance migrations between their feeding grounds and breeding grounds. Every two to four years, a female turtle swims back to the beach where she hatched to lay her own eggs. For some turtles, this journey may be thousands of miles (kilometers) long.

When she reaches her destination, the turtle crawls on shore, scoops a hole in the sand with her hind flippers, and lays from 100 to 200 round eggs. Then she buries them and returns to sea. The eggs hatch about two months later. The hatchlings soon head off to sea, too.

One of the world's most important nesting sites for green sea turtles is Australia's Raine Island. Up to 20,000 female turtles nest here each year.

Boats that fish for shrimp in the Atlantic Ocean and the Gulf of Mexico are required to use "turtle excluder devices," known as TEDs. These devices keep sea turtles from getting trapped in shrimp nets.

A leatherback's mouth is lined with spines that point backward to help the turtle hold on to its gooey jellyfish prey.

After hatching, baby leatherback turtles race down the beach to the sea. Predators such as crabs and seabirds snap up some hatchlings before they reach the water. In the ocean, sharks and other fish eat them, too. Only about one in a thousand hatchlings will survive to adulthood.

LEATHERBACK SEA TURTLE

The leatherback sea turtle is the world's biggest turtle and one of the largest reptiles on Earth.

They can weigh more than 1,320 pounds (600 kg) and measure up to 8 feet (2.4 m) in length. Some, however, grow even larger. The biggest leatherback on record was a male that was 8.5 feet (2.6 m) long and weighed 2,020 pounds (916 kg)—about as much as a small car!

This species is named after the unique structure of its shell. It's made up of a jigsaw puzzle of small bones embedded in tough, oily tissue and covered by leathery skin. The teardrop shape of the carapace and the ridges running down its back make the leatherback "streamlined," which means it's shaped to glide smoothly and swiftly through the water. Power for swimming comes from the leatherback's big, whalelike front flippers.

Leatherbacks have the ability to produce some of their own body heat as they use their muscles. Their big bodies and thick layers of fat help hold in this heat. As a result, they're able to swim in cold ocean waters avoided by other sea turtles. They can also dive deeper than any other turtle—up to 4,200 feet (1,280 m) beneath the waves.

Leatherbacks also make the longest migration of any sea turtle, traveling as far as 3,700 miles (6,000 km) from their feeding ground to the beaches where they themselves hatched to lay their eggs. And all this is accomplished on a diet of mostly jellyfish!

FAMILY
Dermochelyidae

FACTS

OTHER COMMON NAMES
Luth, trunkback, coffin-back, leathery turtle, trunk turtle

SCIENTIFIC NAME
Dermochelys coriacea

SIZE
4–8 feet (1.2–2.4 m)

FOOD
Jellyfish, crustaceans, fish, octopuses

HABITAT
Oceans, coastal waters

RANGE
Worldwide

CROCODILES, ALLIGATORS, CAIMANS, & GHARIALS

ALL ABOUT CROCODYLIANS

Crocodylians, like turtles, belong to an ancient order of reptiles. One of the oldest crocodile fossils dates back 240 million years. So, along with turtles, crocodylians saw the rise and fall of the dinosaurs and their extinction 65 million years ago.

Many people think that crocodylians descended from dinosaurs, but this isn't the case. It's true that crocodylians and dinosaurs shared ancestors called archosaurs, a name that means "ruling reptiles." But archosaurs split into different lines, one of which led to dinosaurs and another to crocodylians.

Today's crocodylians belong to about 23 species.

Crocodylians share adaptations for life as aquatic predators. Their bodies are streamlined, with strong tails used for swimming and webbed hind feet for steering. A flap in the throat stops water from gushing into the croc when it is wrestling with or eating its prey. Their teeth fall out and are replaced throughout their lives, though the replacement process slows down as the croc gets older.

Crocodylians' eyes, ears, and nostrils are positioned on their heads so that they remain above the water when their bodies are submerged. A crocodylian has excellent vision and hearing, and a strong sense of smell.

In the past, crocodylians were viewed as nothing more than vicious killers. Modern research has revealed that they actually live complex social lives. They communicate with others of their kind and have a "pecking order," like many mammals and some birds. Many species guard their nests, help their young hatch, and guard the hatchlings. Crocodylians are thought to be more closely related to birds than they are to other reptiles.

Mugger
(Crocodylus palustris)
The Asian "mugger" crocodile's name comes from a word that means "water monster" in a language spoken in India.

Cuban crocodile
(Crocodylus rhombifer)
The Cuban crocodile is an endangered species found in just two swamplands in Cuba.

Dwarf crocodile
(Osteolaemus tetraspis)
The dwarf crocodile of Africa can be up to 6.5 feet (2 m) long.

Slender-snouted crocodile
(Mecistops cataphractus)
Slender-snouted crocodiles are excellent swimmers, but they can often be found resting on tree branches close to water.

Spectacled caiman
(Caiman crocodilus)
The spectacled caiman of Central and South America is named for the bony ridge between its eyes.

False gharial
(Tomistoma schlegelii)
The false gharial of Southeast Asia has from 76 to 84 teeth in its long, skinny snout.

233

Alligator hatchlings are about 6 to 8 inches (15–20 cm) long and can safely hitch a ride in their mother's jaws! Female alligators stay with their young for up to two years.

American alligators may go dormant for as long as five months in colder, northern parts of their range. They hide from the cold in burrows called gator holes.

AMERICAN ALLIGATOR

The American alligator is the largest reptile in North America. One giant gator caught in the past was recorded as being about 19 feet (6 m) long! Males are bigger and heavier than females and can weigh up to 1,000 pounds (454 kg). Only the American crocodile (pages 242–243) rivals the gator in size.

This big reptile has thick, leathery skin paved with bony plates called osteoderms. Its powerful jaws seize prey ranging from fish to deer. Its mouth is lined with as many as 80 teeth, which are replaced when they wear out or are lost. An alligator may run through nearly 3,000 teeth in the course of its life!

These teeth, however, aren't used for chewing—the alligator swallows its food in chunks. Small animals are swallowed whole; bigger animals are shaken so that they break into smaller portions. The alligator may also hang on to its meal and spin like a top to twist off pieces. Its strong stomach acids can digest tough materials such as bones and turtle shells.

Alligators were once an endangered species. By the early 1960s, their numbers had dropped steeply after decades of being hunted for their skins, which were used to make leather. Alligators disappeared from areas where they were once common. Many people feared the alligator would become extinct. Strict laws that controlled the hunting of alligators were passed. Over time, alligator populations started to recover. Today, scientists estimate there are about 5 million American alligators in the wild.

FAMILY
Alligatoridae

FACTS

OTHER COMMON NAMES
Mississippi alligator, gator

SCIENTIFIC NAME
Alligator mississippiensis

SIZE
10–15 feet (3–4.6 m)

FOOD
Fish, snails, crabs, frogs, snakes, turtles, birds, mammals

HABITAT
Freshwater rivers, lakes, swamps, ponds, marshes, rivers, bayous

RANGE
Southeastern United States and parts of Texas

CHINESE ALLIGATOR

FAMILY
Alligatoridae

There are only two species of alligators: the American alligator (pages 234–235) and the Chinese alligator, which is half its size and lives half a world away.

Chinese alligators behave very much like their American cousins. In winter, they go dormant and lie low in burrows. In spring, courtship begins, and females later build and guard nests. They also carry their young to water in their mouths. Unlike the burrows of American alligators, Chinese alligator burrows are complex systems. They have air holes throughout, and they may connect with pools above the ground. They might also feature underground pools! A burrow system may be home to more than one gator.

Unlike the American alligator, the Chinese species is critically endangered. Hunting and habitat loss have caused its near disappearance. Today, only about 130 Chinese alligators live in the wild. Efforts to protect wild populations didn't stop the decline, so China began a captive breeding program. Some of the young alligators raised in captivity have been released into the wild to start new populations. China is also working to restore wetlands that had been turned into farmlands so they can be used as habitats for alligators, too.

FACTS

OTHER COMMON NAMES
Yangtze alligator, *yow lung* ("dragon")

SCIENTIFIC NAME
Alligator sinensis

SIZE
5–6.5 feet (1.5–2 m)

FOOD
Insects, clams, snails, fish, birds, small mammals

HABITAT
Ponds, lakes, rivers, streams, marshes, swamps, farm ditches

RANGE
Central coast of eastern China, near Yangtze River

Zoos around the world breed this endangered species. In 2007, alligators from New York's Bronx Zoo were released into the wild in China along with hatchlings from other zoos. The reintroduced alligators settled in quickly and were reproducing by 2008.

A Chinese alligator's eyelids contain bony plates. American alligators' eyelids don't.

237

The black caiman is the biggest species in the alligator family.

Black caiman hatchlings have white or yellow bands on their sides and gray stripes on their jaws. Adult black caimans wear a slightly duller version of these markings.

BLACK CAIMAN

Caimans are in the same family as alligators.

They look similar, but caimans have shorter tails than alligators do, and their snouts are more pointed. Caimans live in Central and South America, and the biggest of them is the black caiman.

Black caimans eat a variety of animals, but they feed primarily on fish. Fierce fish called piranha, which have razor-sharp teeth, are among their favorites. They also eat a dog-size rodent called the capybara. Really big caimans have been known to tackle tapirs and anacondas!

The black caiman has disappeared across much of its range in the past 50 years. Starting in the 1940s, people began hunting this species heavily for its dark skin, which was used to make shiny black leather. Scientists estimate that its numbers dropped by 99 percent. As a result, farmers have noticed an increase in the numbers of capybara, which feed on their crops.

Today, black caimans are protected by law, and areas of their habitat are being protected. Captive breeding programs have been put in place to rebuild wild populations.

FAMILY
Alligatoridae

FACTS

OTHER COMMON NAMES
Jacare-assu

SCIENTIFIC NAME
Melanosuchus niger

SIZE
13–20 feet (4–6 m)

FOOD
Mollusks, fish, frogs, reptiles, birds, mammals

HABITAT
Freshwater rivers, lakes, swamps, streams, wetlands

RANGE
Northern South America

DWARF CAIMAN

The dwarf caiman is widely considered to be the world's smallest crocodylian (though Africa is home to dwarf crocodiles that are almost the same size). Males of this species can grow to be 5 feet (1.5 m) long, about the length of a typical bicycle. In some parts of Brazil, however, some dwarf caimans are reported to grow up to 6 feet (1.8 m) long.

Dwarf caimans are widespread, and they're not endangered. Their hides are studded with many bony, thick osteoderms, which makes them unsuitable for use as leather—and this has saved their lives because they haven't been hunted for their skins. People in parts of South America hunt dwarf caimans for food and also eat their eggs, but this small amount of hunting poses no threat to the population of dwarf caimans.

The dwarf caiman and its "cousin," the Schneider's dwarf caiman, are the most heavily armored of the crocodylians. They probably need extra-strong armor because of their small size. Young dwarf caimans are eaten by snakes, birds, and rats, while adults are hunted by jaguars and big snakes, such as the green anaconda (pages 134–135).

The dwarf caiman has a unique head shape. The snout is short, and the skull is tall instead of flattened. It is often compared to the skull of a dog.

A dwarf caiman's sharp, curved teeth help it catch fish in fast-moving water.

The American crocodile is a shy, timid animal. There is only one incident on record of an American crocodile biting people in the United States. The croc most likely bit the swimmers thinking they were prey. (The people were injured but survived.)

CROCODILE

You can quickly tell an American crocodile and an American alligator apart by looking at their heads. A crocodile's snout is more pointed than an alligator's. You can also see the fourth tooth on either side of a crocodile's lower jaw sticking out when the croc's mouth is shut.

ALLIGATOR

AMERICAN CROCODILE

If you see a crocodylian in the U.S. state of Florida, it's almost always an American alligator (pages 234–235). But if you travel all the way to Florida's southern tip, where the state comes to a point between the Gulf of Mexico and the rest of the Atlantic Ocean—and if you're really lucky—you might spy an American crocodile.

The American crocodile is the only crocodile species that occurs naturally in the United States. Here, at the very edge of the nation, its range overlaps with that of the southernmost American alligators. It's the only place where both of the United States' croc species meet.

The two reptiles don't compete one-on-one with each other for food and nesting sites, however. American alligators are a freshwater species. They can endure salt water for a while, but it's not their habitat. The American crocodile, on the other hand, is right at home in water that is "brackish"—a mixture of fresh and salty water. It can tolerate salt water, too, which has allowed these crocs to swim from island to island in the Caribbean. Unlike alligators, however, the crocodiles can't survive cold weather, so they'll never live as far north as gators do.

FAMILY
Crocodylidae

OTHER COMMON NAMES
Central American alligator, South American alligator, American saltwater crocodile

SCIENTIFIC NAME
Crocodylus acutus

SIZE
10–20 feet (3–6 m)

FOOD
Fish, crabs, turtles, birds, small mammals

HABITAT
Brackish or saltwater areas; bays, ponds, coves, coastal lagoons, mangrove swamps, river estuaries

RANGE
Mexico, Central America, Caribbean, northern South America, southern tip of Florida

FACTS

NILE CROCODILE

FACTS

OTHER COMMON NAMES
East African Nile crocodile, Kenya crocodile

SCIENTIFIC NAME
Crocodylus niloticus

SIZE
11–20 feet (3.5–6 m)

FOOD
Fish; antelope, warthogs, wildebeest, zebra, and other large mammals

HABITAT
Swamps, marshes, rivers, lakes

RANGE
Africa, Madagascar

A Nile crocodile starts life as a bug-eating, frog-catching hatchling that could fit in a shoebox.
A decade later, it's big enough to eat an African buffalo! This reptile is the largest species of crocodylian in Africa. Males generally reach 16 feet (5 m) in length, but crocs as long as 20 feet (6 m) have been recorded.

A Nile crocodile ambushes its prey, submerging its own body and then lunging at animals that drink at the water's edge. It grabs its prey by the head and drags it into the water. A hungry croc can eat up to half of its weight in one meal.

Nile crocodiles range far and wide in Africa. They also live on the African island of Madagascar, which lies about 250 miles (400 km) east of the continent. Madagascar's crocodiles were nearly wiped out by hunting for the leather trade before laws were put into place to protect them. One population, however, escaped much of the hunting because it lives in an underground maze of chilly, dark caves. Do the crocs live there to escape the hot sun? Do they feed on the caves' eels, bats, and scorpions? How often do they travel out of the caves? Are they a separate species? Scientists are studying the cave crocs to find out answers to these questions and more.

The ancient Egyptians worshiped a crocodile god called Sobek. They made mummies out of Nile crocodiles and buried them to honor Sobek.

A Nile crocodile will eat a hippo calf if it gets a chance, but a hippo mom will defend her calf and can kill a croc with one bite.

Saltwater crocodiles have the most powerful jaws of all crocodylians. Scientists tested the biting strength of each crocodylian species and found that "salties" chomped with a biting power nearly four times stronger than a lion's—enough force to puncture a sheet of metal.

A female saltwater crocodile builds a nest that is a huge mound of mud and plant materials. She guards the nest until the eggs hatch. Then she watches over the hatchlings for a few months, protecting them from predators such as fish, turtles, birds, and bigger crocodiles.

SALTWATER CROCODILE

No living reptile is bigger than the saltwater crocodile. A huge male of this species can measure 23 feet (7 m) from snout to tail and weigh about a ton! One of the biggest saltwater crocodiles ever captured and measured reached 20 feet, 3 inches (6.2 m) in length. It was named Lolong and lived in a zoo in the Philippines from 2011 to 2013. But stories abound of crocodiles past and present measuring even more than that.

The "saltwater" in this croc's name comes from its ability to survive in salty water. This species thrives in brackish water as well as fresh. Saltwater crocs can also travel long distances in the ocean. Recent studies have shown that crocs far out at sea don't spend all their time actively swimming, which would be very tiring. Instead, they drift with currents. Their seafaring talents most likely enabled them to reach new island habitats.

A crocodile this big eats anything it wants, from insects and snakes to warthogs and water buffalo. Seagoing crocs will even eat sharks!

FAMILY
Crocodylidae

OTHER COMMON NAMES
Indo-Pacific crocodile, estuarine crocodile, naked-neck crocodile, saltie

SCIENTIFIC NAME
Crocodylus porosus

SIZE
16–23 feet (5–7 m)

FOOD
Insects, amphibians, crustaceans, fish, reptiles, birds, mammals

HABITAT
Coastal rivers, lakes, swamps, lagoons, estuaries

RANGE
South and Southeast Asia, southwestern Pacific, northern Australia

FACTS

GHARIAL

FAMILY
Gavialidae

OTHER COMMON NAMES
Ganges gharial, Indian gharial, gavial, fish-eating crocodile, long-nosed crocodile

SCIENTIFIC NAME
Gavialis gangeticus

SIZE
12–20 feet (3.5–6 m)

FOOD
Fish, insects, frogs

HABITAT
Rivers

RANGE
India, Nepal

FACTS

The gharial is the only crocodylian of its kind—the sole member of its family. It's also one of the world's biggest crocodylians, rivaling the saltwater crocodile (pages 246–247) in size. Some male gharials have reached lengths of more than 20 feet (6 m).

Despite its size, the gharial poses no danger to people because its long, thin snout is too delicate to handle big prey. Its slim jaws, lined with up to 110 teeth, are specialized for catching fish. The gharial's slender snout can swiftly slice sideways like a sword in the water, enabling it to seize fish with its razor-sharp teeth. To swallow its slippery meal, the gharial lifts its head out of the water and juggles the fish so that it slides down its throat headfirst.

A full-grown male gharial has a large knob on his snout. The knob turns the gharial's hissing sound into a loud buzzing noise. Both the knob and the noise may play a role in gharial courtship.

Gharials were once a plentiful species that lived not only in India and Nepal but also in Pakistan, Myanmar, Bhutan, and Bangladesh. But hunting for the leather trade, the gathering of eggs for food, habitat loss, pollution, and accidental capture in fishing nets have caused their numbers to plummet. Today, only about 200 adult gharials live in the wild. Efforts to save this species include protecting their nests, setting up sanctuaries, and raising them in captivity.

"Gharial" comes from a Hindi word, *ghara,* which means "pot." It refers to the bump on a male gharial's snout, which resembles a kind of pot used for cooking.

The false gharial is a long-snouted, fish-eating crocodile that lives in southeast Asia. It's called "false" because it looks like a gharial but isn't one. Based on new research, however, some scientists think it should be in the same family as the gharial.

249

TUATARAS

ORDER: RHYNCHOCEPHALIA

The tuatara is the only living species in its order and survives only on scattered islands in New Zealand. Rats introduced by people ate tuatara eggs and hatchlings and nearly drove the species to extinction. Today, some islands are once again rat-free and safe for tuataras.

A tuatara chews its food in a way unlike any other living animal. Its lower jaw holds a single row of teeth that fits between two rows of teeth on the upper jaw when the mouth is shut. By sliding its lower jaw back and forth, it slices the food as if cutting it with scissors.

TUATARA

A tuatara has scaly skin, claws, and spikes down its back. It's also "cold-blooded," or ectothermic. Yet even though it looks a lot like a lizard, it isn't one. It is descended from a different group of reptiles than lizards are. Some differences between them are hidden inside, in the shapes of different bones. Other differences are visible on the outside. A tuatara, for example, does not have an external ear opening.

Like some lizards, however, a tuatara has a "third eye" on the top of the head that is sensitive to light levels. It's most visible on the head of a hatchling. Hatchlings keep their other two eyes peeled for predators—including adult tuataras!

A tuatara lives life in the slow lane. It can take 35 years to grow to its full length. It isn't old enough to reproduce until it's 10 to 20 years of age. A female takes about two years to form eggs in her body. Once they're laid, the eggs can take up to 16 months to hatch. No other reptile's eggs take that long to incubate.

This slowness is an adaptation to life in the cool climate of New Zealand's offshore islands. Tuataras burn energy on the "low" setting, so they don't need a lot of heat. A tuatara can be very active at temperatures that would be too cool for most reptiles. And the tuatara has time on its side: It can live from 60 to 100 years or more!

FAMILY
Sphenodontidae

FACTS

OTHER COMMON NAMES
Beak-head, sphenodon

SCIENTIFIC NAME
Sphenodon punctatus

SIZE
18–24 inches (45–61 cm)

FOOD
Worms, insects, spiders, snails, seabird eggs and chicks

HABITAT
Coastal forests, scrublands

RANGE
Islands off New Zealand

Tuataras can dig their own burrows, but they often use the burrows of nesting seabirds instead. They'll move in even if the seabird is currently using it—and make themselves unwelcome by eating its eggs and chicks.

Chain king snake
(Lampropeltis getula)
The eastern king snake of North America is also called a chain snake because of the chainlike markings on its skin.

Hawksbill sea turtle
(Eretmochelys imbricata)
The hawksbill sea turtle uses its hawklike beak to reach into nooks and crannies of coral reefs as it searches for sponges, its main food, and other prey.

Orinoco crocodile
(Crocodylus intermedius)
The endangered Orinoco crocodile is found only in the Orinoco River region of Venezuela and Colombia.

Four-eyed turtle
(Sacalia quadriocellata)
Four-eyed turtles from China have "eye spots" on their heads. Males tend to have green spots. Females have yellow ones.

Hairy viper
(Atheris hispidus)
The hairy viper of Africa has ridged scales that make it look bristly. It's also called the rough-scaled tree viper.

Black tree monitor
(Varanus beccarii)
Black tree monitors of New Guinea have green or yellow spots as hatchlings. They turn black as they grow older.

Cook Strait tuatara
(Sphenodon punctatus)
The tuatara's name comes from the language of the Maori people of New Zealand and means "spiny back."

Emerald tree skink
(Dasia smaragdina)
Emerald tree skinks of Indonesia and the Philippines are often bright green, but they can also be brown or blue.

A TALK WITH HERPETOLOGIST ADAM LEACHÉ

Herpetologists are scientists who study reptiles and amphibians.

Different herpetologists focus their research on different subjects. Some study how reptiles adapt to their habitats. Others study reptile behavior, how reptile bodies work, or how reptile populations rise and fall. And some herpetologists find ways to help conserve endangered reptiles.

Adam Leaché is a herpetologist at the University of Washington in Seattle, Washington, U.S.A. We spoke to Adam to learn more about what herpetologists like him do, and to get some reptile-studying tips.

What do herpetologists do?

Herpetologists work with reptiles and amphibians. There are lots of kinds of jobs for herpetologists. You can teach at a school, work at a museum, or help care for animals at a zoo. Some herpetologists work on conservation projects to protect endangered species. This can involve restoring habitats or raising animals in captivity before releasing them back into nature.

Tell us more about what you do.

I'm a professor of biology at the University of Washington, and a curator at the Burke Museum in Seattle. My jobs allow me to do a lot of different things with reptiles and amphibians.

I teach courses in biology, including introductory biology and herpetology. As a curator, I care for the amphibian and reptile collection, and I also help design exhibits. One of the most important things I do is mentor and train students who want to become professional biologists. Together, we conduct research on reptiles and amphibians. We go on field expeditions to find and collect different species for our research and to bring the samples back to the lab, where we study their DNA to understand their genetic diversity. [Genetic diversity means the variety of genes found in a species. DNA is the substance that makes up the genes.]

What's your favorite reptile?

I've always been fascinated by horned lizards. Their horns are really cool, and they do some of the strangest things imaginable for a lizard. Some species can shoot blood out of their eyes as an anti-predator defense mechanism. They can use their body like a shield so that snakes can't eat them. They can also channel water into their mouths without moving—all they have to do is stand in a puddle or collect rain on their back and it works its way to their mouths. They are also experts at camouflage.

What do you find most fascinating about reptiles?

Reptiles have to find creative ways to regulate their body temperature to remain active. It's easy for mammals like us to be active all the time, because we generate our own body heat. This is one of the traits that make reptiles so distinct from other animals. When I was a kid, I learned that reptiles are "cold-blooded," but this term doesn't always make sense. Some species of lizards are most active when the temperature of their blood is over 100°F [38°C]. There's nothing "cold" about that!

What advice would you give to kids who want to study reptiles?

The best way to start studying reptiles is to watch them in the wild. This means going out to a natural area and observing them. Once you find them, follow them as they hunt for food and interact with other species. Take notes on what you find. You never know when you might discover something new.

When you find a reptile, what do you look for as you try to identify it—especially if it's an unfamiliar species?

Many species of reptiles can be distinguished by their color or pattern, but the key to identifying some species is to study their scales. This often requires catching the animal and inspecting the scales very closely, and sometimes counting the number of scales in certain parts of the body. With snakes, the first thing we do is determine whether or not it is venomous before we touch it.

How much time have you devoted to studying a particular reptile?

I've devoted over ten years to studying African agama lizards. It took that long to collect all the species living in different parts of the continent. Most of my research is on lizards, including horned lizards and spiny lizards in North America, and geckos and agama lizards in Africa.

Have you ever discovered a new reptile species?

I've discovered and described new species of lizards, and a few frogs, too. Sometimes you know that a species is new as soon as you find it, but other times you don't realize that you've found a new species until you've brought it back to the lab and compared it to other species.

What tips can you offer for kids who want to observe reptiles in their backyard or local parks?

The key to observing reptiles is to keep a close eye on them. Don't get so close that they try to escape from you. If you want to see the reptile in action, then you have to watch it from a distance. Another important piece of advice is to stay away from snakes that you can't identify. You absolutely don't want to get bitten by a venomous snake!

HOW YOU CAN HELP

According to the IUCN (International Union for Conservation of Nature), about 19 percent of the world's reptiles are in danger of becoming extinct. What can you do to help stop their decline?

Reduce, Reuse, Recycle

Recycling an aluminum can, fixing a leaky faucet, or bringing a reusable bag to the grocery store don't sound like activities that can help reptiles. But these everyday choices are small actions that can add up to make a big impact. Take that aluminum can, for example: It can be melted down and used to make new cans using just a fraction of the energy it takes to dig up and refine a new batch of aluminum. Saving energy and materials helps protect habitat because it slows down the rate at which we humans dig and drill in those habitats.

In the same way, when you use a reusable cloth bag for shopping instead of a plastic bag from the store, you're helping to reduce the amount of energy and raw materials used to make plastic bags. Your choice even has a more direct link to saving reptiles than you might think! Plastic bags often end up in the ocean when they're blown off the street or out of garbage cans into storm drains, which drain into waterways. Leatherback sea turtles (pages 228–229), which feed on jellyfish, mistake the bags for their prey and eat them—a mistake that sickens and slowly kills them.

Join an Organization or Project

Spreading the news about endangered reptiles raises public awareness of the issue. Check with a local nature center or science museum to see if they have a club or project focusing on reptiles, a community project to restore reptile habitat, or a citizen-science project that needs volunteers. There are also citizen-science projects based online that seek data from near and far, and many of them welcome participation by kids. The Center for Snake Conservation, for example, invites citizens to submit sightings of snakes and conducts yearly snake counts on their website (www.snakecount.org). Try using search terms such as "kids," "citizen science," and "reptiles" to find others.

You can also help win over people's hearts and minds and capture their interest simply by sharing the wonder of reptiles and other wildlife. Some of these projects can be found online, such as National Geographic's Great Nature Project (www.greatnatureproject.org), which invites people from around the world to take pictures of animals and plants and then share them online.

Pick Up the Trash

Help keep your neighborhood, forests, and parks clean. Put on a pair of gloves to pick up trash and discourage "litterbugs" from doing further damage. You can also help cut down on litter at its source by buying fewer products that use a lot of packaging. For example, you can buy fruit that's sold loose in bins instead of in plastic packaging, and fill a reusable bottle with water instead of buying bottled water.

Curb Global Climate Change

According to scientists, burning fossil fuels, such as oil and gasoline, releases heat-trapping gases into the atmosphere. The result is global climate change—a change in Earth's climate. This phenomenon threatens reptiles in many ways. One study, for example, showed that declining populations of some lizards could be due to higher springtime temperatures, which drove lizards to spend more time in the shade and less time looking for food at a time of year when females need lots of nutrients in order to produce young. This change in behavior could make lizard populations drop. It may seem as if this is too big a problem for an ordinary person to tackle, but actually every bit of effort helps: You can help reduce the burning of fossil fuels by turning off lights when you leave a room, replacing traditional lightbulbs with fluorescent bulbs, putting on a sweater instead of turning up the heat, and towel drying your hair instead of blow-drying it.

Leave Reptiles in the Wild

Sometimes a lizard, turtle, or harmless snake is easily captured in the wild. Briefly observe the reptile and set it free even if it's tempting to take it home for a pet. First, it may be protected by law, and second, the reptile is better off in its natural habitat. In addition, reptiles are not easy to keep in captivity. If you're a budding herpetologist and wish to keep a reptile, make sure that you purchase a reptile that was captive-bred. Many species of reptile are illegally caught in the wild for sale as pets, and some species are teetering on the brink of extinction as a result of this activity. Millions of reptiles are illegally captured and then shipped between countries each year under horrific conditions. According to the Animal Legal and Historical Center, about 90 percent of the survivors die in their first year as pets.

Don't Buy Reptiles as Souvenirs

Unfortunately, in some parts of the world reptiles and their body parts are made into souvenirs for sale to tourists. These souvenirs range from purses made out of the heads and limbs of crocodiles to stuffed lizards and turtle-shell rattles. If you are part of a traveling family, bring home some other souvenir instead.

259

GLOSSARY

ADAPTATION — a feature that helps a living organism survive in its environment

AMPHIBIAN — a cold-blooded animal that lacks scales. Most amphibians start life in water in a juvenile form that gradually changes into an adult form. A frog, for example, is an amphibian that starts out as a legless tadpole and changes into a four-legged adult as it grows. Other amphibians include newts, salamanders, and toads.

BRUMATING — hibernating. Herpetologists often use this term to describe the winter dormancy of reptiles.

CAMOUFLAGE — an organism's ability to disguise its appearance, often by using its coloring or body shape to blend in with its surroundings. An example is a lizard that looks like a leaf.

CARAPACE — the upper portion of a turtle's shell. It is joined to the bottom part, the plastron, along the sides of the body.

CARRION — the decaying flesh of a dead animal

CASQUE — the helmetlike portion of a chameleon's head. Casques range in size from flattened bumps to tall peaks.

CHROMATOPHORES — cells in a reptile's body that produce its skin colors. Some colors are produced by pigments in the cells, while others contain substances with structures that reflect light to produce color.

CLOACA — the opening in the hind end of a reptile used for both reproduction and expelling waste from the body

COMMON NAME — the non-scientific name of an organism that is used by a community of people. Not all common names are the same in all regions. For example, the collared lizard is known as a "mountain boomer" in some regions.

CONVERGENT EVOLUTION — the process in which animals that are not related and live in different parts of the world evolve similar adaptations

COURTSHIP — a behavior used by animals to attract each other for mating

DEFENSE — a means by which an organism protects itself from attack or harm. Defenses can be part of an animal's body (for example, its spines), part of its coloring, part of its chemistry (a rattlesnake can inject venom with its teeth), or its behavior (it can hide).

DEWLAP — a flap of skin on a reptile's throat that is used for communication and display

ECTOTHERM — an animal that is dependent on the temperature of its surroundings to control its body temperature. A lizard, for example, may bask in the sun to raise its body temperature and hide in a burrow to cool down.

ENDANGERED — relating to an animal or plant that is found in such small numbers that it is at risk of becoming extinct, or no longer existing

ENDOTHERM — an animal, such as a mammal, with a body that is able to generate its own heat regardless of the temperature of its surroundings

ENVIRONMENT — the natural features of a place, such as its weather, the kind of land it has, and the type of plants that grow in it

ESTIVATING — going into a state of inactivity within a protected place during hot seasons when food and water may be scarce. Reptiles also estivate to avoid high temperatures that would cause their bodies to overheat.

EXTINCTION — the state of no longer existing, or being alive. When all the members of a species die out, they are said to go extinct.

FOSSIL — the preserved remains or traces of an organism that lived a long time ago

HABITAT — a place in nature where an organism lives throughout the year, or for shorter periods of time

HERPETOLOGIST — a scientist who studies reptiles, amphibians, or both

HIBERNACULA — dens where many reptiles of the same species gather to hibernate. Sometimes a hibernaculum may contain several species.

HIBERNATING — going into a state of inactivity within a protected place during winter. Reptiles that hibernate do not eat or move around until warmer temperatures return. Reptile hibernation is also called brumation.

INVASIVE SPECIES — species that are introduced accidentally or on purpose from their native habitat to a new location. Also called "introduced species" or "exotic species." Invasive species typically have a bad effect on native plants and animals.

INVERTEBRATE — an organism without a backbone. Invertebrates include insects, arachnids, crustaceans, and mollusks.

MEASUREMENT — the length, height, width, or weight of something. In most areas of the world, the metric system is the preferred system of measurement, while in the United States, U.S. standard units are used. Some common units of measurement include:

1 millimeter (mm) = 0.04 inches (in.)
1 centimeter (cm) = 0.4 inches (in.)
1 meter (m) = 3.3 feet (ft.)
1 kilometer (km) = 3,281 feet (ft.)
1 gram (g) = 0.04 ounces (oz.)
1 kilogram (kg) = 2.2 pounds (lb.)

MIGRATION — the seasonal movement from one location to another. The migration may be prompted by various environmental cues, including weather and availability of food. Sea turtles and garter snakes are examples of reptiles that migrate.

OSTEODERM — bony plates in the skin of some reptiles, such as alligators

OVIPAROUS — producing young by laying eggs in which embryos develop into live young that hatch

PATAGIUM — the skin stretched across the ribs of certain species of flying reptiles that gives them the ability to glide

PIT ORGANS — holes in the face of a snake that detect the body heat of another animal and help the snake "see" its prey in the dark. Pit vipers, such as rattlesnakes, have pit organs that lie partway down the face between the eyes and the nostrils. Pythons and boas have pit organs along their lips.

PLASTRON — the bottom portion of a turtle's shell. It is joined to the upper part, the carapace, along the sides of the body.

PREDATOR — an animal that hunts other animals for food. Its behavior is "predatory."

PREY — an animal that is hunted and eaten by other animals

RAIN FOREST — an evergreen forest with upwards of 160 inches (406 cm) of rain in a year. There are both tropical and temperate rain forests.

REPTILE CLASSIFICATION — the grouping of reptiles based on their relatedness and their physical characteristics. For example, the class Reptilia (reptiles) is divided into orders (such as Crocodylia, or crocodiles, alligators, caimans, and the gharial). The order is divided into families. Each family is divided into genera (the plural of genus), and each genus is divided into species. (In some cases, there is only one member of a family or genus.) The species has a double name that is italicized. The first name is the genus name followed by a species name.

SCIENTIFIC NAME — a unique two-part name used by scientists to identify each type of organism. Most scientific names come from Latin or Greek. For example, *Agama agama* is the scientific name for the rainbow agama. There are other related species of lizards in the genus *Agama* (each with a double name starting with *Agama*), and in turn they are part of the lizard family Agamidae, which in turn is in the order Squamata, which consists of all lizards, snakes, and worm lizards.

SPECTACLE — the clear scale that covers the eyes of snakes and some lizards. It is also called a brille.

TEMPERATE ZONE — that part of the Earth's surface located between the tropics and the polar regions. The temperate zone is characterized by a warm summer and a cool winter.

TERRITORIAL — relating to animals that carefully guard an area considered to be their own. For example, a male saltwater crocodile will attack other males that enter the area of water that he has claimed as his territory to prevent them from mating with females in that territory.

THERMOREGULATION — the ability of an organism to control its body temperature

TROPICAL ZONE — the part of the Earth's surface surrounding the Equator. The tropics are characterized by a hot climate year round.

VENOM — a toxic substance produced by a reptile's body and injected into other animals by biting. A venomous reptile is one that produces venom.

VERTEBRATE — an organism with a backbone. Vertebrates include mammals, fish, reptiles, amphibians, and birds.

VIVIPAROUS — giving birth to live young

FIND OUT MORE

Great Websites, Movies, and Places to Visit

WEBSITES

Find loads of photos, videos, and information about reptiles at National Geographic's "Reptiles" website: animals.nationalgeographic.com/animals/reptiles

The website for *Reptiles* magazine is packed with information about reptiles, including how to care for them—and you'll often find contests here, too! www.reptilesmagazine.com

The San Diego Zoo's website includes a fact-packed introduction to reptiles, as well as in-depth sections about each reptile order: animals.sandiegozoo.org/content/reptiles

More than 10,000 species of reptile are included on the website of the Reptile Database: www.reptile-database.org

To learn about issues related to endangered reptiles and amphibians, check out the website of the Amphibian and Reptile Conservancy: amphibianandreptileconservancy.org

Information about and photos of reptiles are available on the University of Michigan's BioKids website: www.biokids.umich.edu/critters/Reptilia

Learn about the National Zoo's reptile exhibits, and reptile conservation and adaptations, on the zoo's website: nationalzoo.si.edu/animals/reptilesamphibians/exhibit/default.cfm

Videos and photos of reptiles abound on ARKive's website: www.arkive.org/reptiles

The St. Louis Zoo devotes part of its website to everything reptilian: www.stlzoo.org/animals/abouttheanimals/reptiles

The Encyclopedia of Life website offers information and images of reptiles on their website: eol.org/info/441

BBC Nature has pictures and information about more than 80 species of reptile on its website: www.bbc.co.uk/nature/life/Reptile/by/rank/all

MOVIES

BBC

Dragons Alive (2004): Reptile evolution, adaptation, and conservation are covered in this three-part documentary.

Life in Cold Blood (2008): This five-part series includes both reptiles and amphibians, and it explores their adaptations, diversity, and behavior.

NATURE

Invasion of the Giant Pythons (2010): Burmese pythons that have escaped or been released into the wetlands of Florida, U.S.A., are feeding on the native wildlife. How will this affect the life and habitat of Everglades National Park?

The Reptiles (2003): This four-part series devotes entire episodes to crocodylians, lizards, snakes, and turtles.

Supersize Crocs (2007): In this documentary, a crocodile conservationist scours the globe to find the last living giant individuals of different crocodylian species.

NOVA

Arctic Dinosaurs (2011): Scientists journey across Alaska, U.S.A., to study fossil beds containing 70-million-year-old bones, which tell the story of dinosaurs that survived in polar regions.

"Australia's First 4 Billion Years: Monsters" (2013): This episode in a four-part series presents the large and dangerous reptiles that once ruled the land that is now Australia.

Lizard Kings (2009): This documentary focuses on the mighty monitors, a family of lizards that includes the fierce Komodo dragon.

Venom: Nature's Killer (2011): Scientists study some of the world's most venomous animals, including many reptiles, to see if their chemicals hold cures.

PLACES TO VISIT

U.S.A.

Reptile House, Sacramento Zoo, California

Reptile House and Reptile Walk, San Diego Zoo, California

Alligator Farm Zoological Park, St. Augustine, Florida

Scaly Slimy Spectacular: The Amphibian and Reptile Experience, Zoo Atlanta, Georgia

HerpAquarium, Louisville Zoo, Kentucky

Reptile Encounter, Audubon Zoo, New Orleans, Louisiana

Holden Reptile Conservation Center, Detroit Zoo, Michigan

American International Rattlesnake Museum, Albuquerque, New Mexico

Reptile House, Rio Grande Zoo, Albuquerque, New Mexico

Fear Zone, Staten Island Zoo, New York

World of Reptiles, Bronx Zoo, New York

Reptile Habitat, Columbus Zoo and Aquarium, Ohio

Reptile House, Cincinnati Zoo, Cincinnati, Ohio

Reptile and Amphibian House, Philadelphia Zoo, Philadelphia, Pennsylvania

Reptile Gardens, Rapid City, South Dakota

Amphibian and Reptile Conservation Center, Knoxville Zoo, Knoxville, Tennessee

Museum of Living Art, Fort Worth Zoo, Texas

Reptile Discovery Center, National Zoo, Washington, D.C.

Outside U.S.A.:

CANADA

Prehistoric Park, Calgary Zoo, Calgary, Alberta

Indian River Reptile Zoo, Indian River, Ontario

Little Ray's Reptile Zoo, Ottawa, Ontario

CENTRAL AND SOUTH AMERICA

Reptile House, Buenos Aires Zoo, Argentina

Galápagos Exhibit and Reptile Exhibit, Bermuda Aquarium, Museum, and Zoo, Flatts Village, Bermuda

São Paulo Zoo, Brazil

Parque Reptilandia, Costa Rica

The Herpetarium, Guadalajara Zoo, Jalisco, Mexico

EUROPE

Reptile Zoo, Haus der Natur, Salzburg, Austria (http://www.hausdernatur.at/reptile-zoo.html)

Aquarium, Schönbrunn Zoo, Vienna, Austria (http://www.zoovienna.at/en/zoo-and-visitors/visitor-information/)

The Terrarium, Prague Zoo, Czech Republic (http://www.zoopraha.cz/en)

Reptile House, London Zoo, England (http://www.zsl.org/zsl-london-zoo/exhibits/reptile-house)

The Venomous House, Budapest Zoo, Hungary (http://www.zoobudapest.com/en/must-see/animal-kingdom/venomous-house)

House of Reptiles, Dublin Zoo, Ireland (http://www.dublinzoo.ie/87/House-of-Reptiles.aspx)

Reptile House, Bioparco de Roma, Rome, Italy (http://www.bioparco.it/english/)

Reptile House, Krakow Zoo, Poland (http://www.zoo-krakow.pl/index_en.php)

The Terrarium, Moscow Zoo, Russia (http://www.zoo.ru/moscow/frame_e4.htm)

Reptile House, Barcelona Zoo, Spain (https://www.zoobarcelona.cat/en/know-the-zoo/spaces-in-the-zoo/highlights/reptile-house/)

Interaction with Reptiles, Zoo Aquarium of Madrid, Spain (http://www.zoomadrid.com/interacciones/interaccion-con-reptiles)

The Vivarium, Basel Zoo, Switzerland (http://www.zoobasel.com/en/tiere/anlagen/anlage.php?AnlagenID=4)

ASIA

Reptile House, National Zoological Park, New Delhi, India (http://nzpnewdelhi.gov.in/index.htm)

Reptile House and crocodile enclosure, Arignar Anna Zoological Park, Tamil Nadu, India (http://www.aazoopark.in/)

Ragunan Zoological Park, Jakarta, Indonesia (http://ragunanzoo.jakarta.go.id/)

Vivarium, Ueno Zoological Gardens, Tokyo, Japan (http://www.tokyo-zoo.net/english/ueno/index.html)

Reptile Garden, Singapore Zoo, Singapore (http://www.zoo.com.sg/exhibits-zones/reptile-garden.html#ad-image-0)

Amphibian and Reptile House, Taipei Zoo, Taiwan (http://english.zoo.taipei.gov.tw/ct.asp?xItem=988632&ctNode=23655&mp=104032)

AFRICA

Reptile House, Giza Zoo, Cairo, Egypt (http://www.gizazoo-eg.com/)

Reptile Park, National Zoological Gardens of South Africa, Pretoria, South Africa (http://www.nzg.ac.za/index.php)

Uganda Wildlife Education Centre, Entebbe, Uganda (http://www.uweczoo.org/)

AUSTRALIA

Australian Reptile Park and Wildlife Sanctuary, Somersby, New South Wales (http://www.reptilepark.com.au/)

Reptile World, Taronga Zoo, Sydney, New South Wales (http://taronga.org.au/)

Alice Springs Reptile Centre, Alice Springs, Northern Territory (http://www.reptilecentre.com.au/)

The Crocoseum, Australia Zoo, Beerwah, Queensland (http://www.australiazoo.com.au/visit-us/exhibits/the-crocoseum/)

Reptile House, Adelaide Zoo, Adelaide, South Australia (http://www.zoossa.com.au/adelaide-zoo/zoo-information/zoo-map)

Reptile House, Melbourne Zoo, Melbourne, Victoria (http://www.zoo.org.au/melbourne)

Reptile Encounter, Perth Zoo, South Perth, Western Australia (http://perthzoo.wa.gov.au/)

NEW ZEALAND

Tuatara house, Hamilton Zoo, Hamilton, New Zealand (http://hamiltonzoo.co.nz/)

Hero HQ, Wellington Zoo, Wellington, New Zealand (http://www.wellingtonzoo.com)

INDEX

PHOTO CREDITS

CREDITS

Staff for This Book
Amy Briggs and Priyanka Lamichhane, *Senior Editors*
Susan Bishansky, *Project Editor*
Amanda Larsen, *Art Director*
Angela Terry, *Designer*
Lori Epstein, *Senior Photo Editor*
Jen Agresta, *Fact-checker*
Paige Towler, *Editorial Assistant*
Sanjida Rashid and Rachel Kenny, *Design Production Assistants*
Michael Cassady, *Rights Clearance Specialist*
Grace Hill, *Managing Editor*
Alix Inchausti, *Production Editor*
Lewis R. Bassford, *Production Manager*
George Bounelis, *Manager, Production Services*
Susan Borke, *Legal and Business Affairs*

Published by the National Geographic Society
Gary E. Knell, *President and CEO*
John M. Fahey, *Chairman of the Board*
Melina Gerosa Bellows, *Chief Education Officer*
Declan Moore, *Chief Media Officer*
Hector Sierra, *Senior Vice President and General Manager, Book Division*

Senior Management Team, Kids Publishing and Media
Nancy Laties Feresten, *Senior Vice President;* Jennifer Emmett, *Vice President, Editorial Director, Kids Books;* Julie Vosburgh Agnone, *Vice President, Editorial Operations;* Rachel Buchholz, *Editor and Vice President,* NG Kids *magazine;* Michelle Sullivan, *Vice President, Kids Digital;* Eva Absher-Schantz, *Design Director;* Jay Sumner, *Photo Director;* Hannah August, *Marketing Director;* R. Gary Colbert, *Production Director*

Digital Anne McCormack, *Director;* Laura Goertzel, Sara Zeglin, *Producers;* Emma Rigney, *Creative Producer;* Bianca Bowman, *Assistant Producer;* Natalie Jones, *Senior Product Manager*

For more information, please visit nationalgeographic.com, call 1-800-NGS LINE (647-5463), or write to the following address:

National Geographic Society
1145 17th Street N.W.
Washington, D.C. 20036-4688 U.S.A.

Visit us online at nationalgeographic.com/books

For librarians and teachers: ngchildrensbooks.org

More for kids from National Geographic:
kids.nationalgeographic.com

For information about special discounts for bulk purchases, please contact National Geographic Books Special Sales: ngspecsales@ngs.org

For rights or permissions inquiries, please contact National Geographic Books Subsidiary Rights: ngbookrights@ngs.org

Hardcover ISBN: 978-1-4263-2102-3
Reinforced library binding ISBN: 978-1-4263-2103-0

Printed in Hong Kong
15/THK/1